# Scope and Trends of Research on Teaching

# Scope and Trends of Research on Teaching

Hemlata Talesra

AUTHORSPRESS

Worldwide Circulation through Authorspress Global Network
First Published 2004
by Authorspress

E-35/103, Jawahar Park
Laxmi Nagar, Delhi-110 092

e-mail: authorspress@yahoo.com



Typeset in NewCenturySchlbk by Chitra Computers

*Scope and Trends of Research on Teaching*
ISBN 81-7273-189-2

Printed in India at Tarun Offset, Delhi.

# Preface

Young people are part of a rapidly changing knowledge society where they will need sound general education, good communication skills, flexibility and adaptability to continue their learning throughout their lives. The ability to access and generate new knowledge in a purposeful fashion, and the need to move beyond content to critical analysis and an understanding of emerging trends and issues, places great demands on our education and training systems to deliver not simply specific skills and knowledge, but also the attitudes and aptitudes to sustain learning throughout life.

The role of the teacher is progressively being broadened from that of the expert who imparts knowledge to one that includes mentor or guide—one who extends students' deep understandings and facilitates the acquisition of higher order thinking skills and creative problem solving skills—skills that are critical for the development of an innovative culture for tomorrow.

Substantive changes in education is unlikely to occur until educators understand how each teacher's beliefs about the nature of teaching and learning, and the metaphors they use to describe their teaching influence everything that occurs in the classroom. This book examines those issues and more. It attempts to locate research on teaching within broader and more inclusive frameworks of current social and philosophical thinking. It is written for students of and scholars in research on teaching. Its contents will also encourage teacher's to probe the realms of subjective experience—the beliefs, values, presuppositions, and metaphors that shape their personal world.

***Editor***

# Contents

# 1

# Qualitative Educational Research

Qualitative research, broadly defined, means "any kind of research that produces findings not arrived at by means of statistical procedures or other means of quantification". Where quantitative researchers seek causal determination, prediction, and generalisation of findings, qualitative researchers seek instead illumination, understanding, and extrapolation to similar situations.

Qualitative analysis results in a different type of knowledge than does quantitative inquiry. E. W. Eisner points out that all knowledge, including that gained through quantitative research, is referenced in qualities, and that there are many ways to represent our understanding of the world: There is a kind of continuum that moves from the fictional that is "true"—the novel for example—to the highly controlled and quantitatively described scientific experiment. Qualitative research and evaluation are located toward the fictive end of the continuum without being fictional in the narrow sense of the term.

Qualitative inquiry accepts the complex and dynamic quality of the social world. There are several considerations when deciding to adopt a qualitative research methodology. Qualitative methods can be used to better understand any phenomenon about which little is yet known. Thus, qualitative methods are appropriate in situations where one needs to first identify the variables that might later be tested quantitatively, or where the researcher has determined that quantitative measures cannot adequately describe or interpret a situation.

## Characteristics of Qualitative Research

Qualitative research reports, typically rich with detail and insights into participants' experiences of the world, "may be epistemologically in harmony with the reader's experience" and thus more meaningful. Several writers have identified what they consider to be the prominent characteristics of qualitative, or naturalistic, research.

i) Qualitative research uses the natural setting as the source of data.

ii) The researcher acts as the "human instrument" of data collection.

iii) Qualitative researchers predominantly use inductive data analysis.

iv) Qualitative research reports are descriptive, incorporating expressive language and the "presence of voice in the text".

v) Qualitative research has an interpretive character, aimed at discovering the meaning that events have for the individuals who experience them, and the interpretations of those meanings by the researcher.

vi) Qualitative researchers pay attention to the idiosyncratic as well as the pervasive, seeking the uniqueness of each case.

vii) Qualitative research has an emergent (as opposed to predetermined) design, and researchers focus on this emerging process as well as the outcomes or product of the research.

viii) Qualitative research is judged using special criteria for trustworthiness.

These characteristics are considered to be "interconnected" and "mutually reinforcing". It is important to emphasise the emergent nature of qualitative research design. Since the researcher seeks to observe and interpret meanings in context, it is neither possible nor appropriate to finalise research strategies before data collection has begun.

Qualitative research proposals should, however, specify primary questions to be explored and plans for data collection strategies. The particular design of a qualitative study depends on the purpose of the inquiry, what information will be most useful, and what information will have the most credibility. There are no strict criteria for sample size. Judgments about usefulness and credibility are left to the researcher and the reader. Before conducting a qualtitative study, a researcher must do three things:

i) the researcher must adopt the stance suggested by the characteristics of the naturalist paradigm.

ii) the researcher must develop the level of skill appropriate for a human instrument, or the vehicle through which data will be collected and interpreted.

iii) the researcher must prepare a research design that utilises accepted strategies for naturalistic inquiry.

**Concept of "Theoretical Sensitivity"**

Theoretical sensitivity refers to a personal quality of the researcher. It indicates an awareness of the subtleties of meaning of data. A. Strauss and J. Corbin believe that theoretical sensitivity comes from a number of sources, including professional literature, professional experiences, and personal experiences. The credibility of a qualitative research report relies heavily on the confidence readers have in the researcher's ability to be sensitive to the data and to make appropriate decisions in the field.

Humans are responsive to environmental cues, and able to interact with the situation; they have the ability to collect information at multiple levels simultaneously; they are able to perceive situations holistically; they are able to process data as soon as they become available; they can provide immediate feedback and request verification of data; and they can explore atypical or unexpected responses.

In quantitative inquiry, the dominant sampling strategy is probability sampling, which depends on the selection of a random and representative sample from the larger population. The purpose of probability sampling is subsequent generalisation of the research findings to the population. By contrast, purposeful sampling is the dominant strategy in qualitative research. Purposeful sampling seeks information-rich cases which can be studied in depth. M. Q. Patton identifies and describes 16 types of purposeful sampling. These include:

i) extreme or deviant case sampling;
ii) typical case sampling;
iii) maximum variation sampling;
iv) snowball or chain sampling;
v) confirming or disconfirming case sampling;
vi) politically important case sampling;
vii) convenience sampling; and others.

The most useful strategy for the naturalistic approach is maximum variation sampling. This strategy aims at capturing and describing the central themes or principal outcomes that cut across a great deal of participant or programme variation. For small samples a great deal of heterogeneity can be a problem because individual cases are so different from each other. Maximum variation sampling can yield detailed descriptions of each case, in addition to identifying shared patterns that cut across cases.

In spite of the apparent flexibility in purposeful sampling, researchers must be aware of three types of sampling error that can arise in qualitative research. The first relates to distortions caused by insufficient breadth in sampling; the second from distortions introduced by changes over time; and the third from distortions caused by lack of depth in data collection at each site. The two prevailing forms of data collection associated with qualitative inquiry are interviews and observation.

*Interviews*: Qualitative interviews may be used either as the primary strategy for data collection, or in conjunction with observation, document analysis, or other techniques.

Qualitative interviewing utilises open-ended questions that allow for individual variations. Patton writes about three types of qualitative interviewing: (1) informal, conversational interviews; (2) semi-structured interviews; and (3) standardised, open-ended interviews. An interview guide or "schedule" is a list of questions or general topics that the interviewer wants to explore during each interview. Although it is prepared to insure that basically the same information is obtained from each person, there are no predetermined responses, and in semi-structured interviews the interviewer is free to probe and explore within these predetermined inquiry areas.

Interview guides ensure good use of limited interview time; they make interviewing multiple subjects more systematic and comprehensive; and they help to keep interactions focused. In keeping with the flexible nature of qualitative research designs, interview guides can be modified over time to focus attention on areas of particular importance, or to exclude questions the researcher has found to be unproductive for the goals of the research.

A basic decision going into the interview process is how to record interview data. Whether one relies on written notes or a tape recorder appears to be largely a matter of personal preference. For instance, Patton says that a tape recorder is "indispensable". Recordings have the advantage of capturing data more faithfully than hurriedly written notes might, and can make it easier for the researcher to focus on the interview.

*Observations*: The classic form of data collection in naturalistic or field research is observation of participants in the context of a natural scene. Observational data are used for the purpose of description—of settings, activities, people, and the meanings of what is observed from the perspective of the participants. Observation can lead to deeper understandings than interviews alone, because it provides a knowledge of the context in which events occur, and may enable the researcher to see things that participants themselves are not aware of, or that they are unwilling to discuss. A skilled observer is one who is trained in the process of monitoring both verbal and nonverbal cues, and in the use of concrete, unambiguous, descriptive language.

There are several observation strategies available. In some cases it may be possible and desirable for the researcher to watch from outside, without being observed. Another option is to maintain a passive presence, being as unobtrusive as possible and not interacting with participants. A third strategy is to engage in limited interaction, intervening only when further clarification of actions is needed. Or the researcher may exercise more active control over the observation, as in the case of a formal interview, to elicit specific types of information. Finally, the researcher may act as a full participant in the situation, with either a hidden or known identity.

The presence of an observer is likely to introduce a distortion of the natural scene which the researcher must be aware of, and work to minimise. Critical decisions, including the degree to which researcher identity and purposes will be revealed to participants, the length of time spent in the field, and specific observation techniques used, are wholly dependent on the unique set of questions and resources brought to each study.

Field researchers rely most heavily on the use of field notes, which are running descriptions of settings, people, activities, and sounds. Field notes may include drawings or maps. In addition to field notes, researchers may use photographs, videotapes, and audio tapes as means of accurately capturing a setting.

Qualitative researchers have few strict guidelines for when to stop the data collection process. Criteria include: (1) exhaustion of resources; (2) emergence of regularities; and (3) overextension, or going too far beyond the boundaries of the research. The decision to stop sampling must take into account the research goals, the need to achieve depth through triangulation of data sources, and the possibility of greater breadth through examination of a variety of sampling sites. Qualitative researchers tend to use inductive analysis of data, meaning that the critical themes emerge out of the data.

Qualitative analysis requires some creativity, for the challenge is to place the raw data into logical, meaningful categories; to examine them in a holistic fashion; and to find a way to communicate this interpretation to others. The mechanics of handling large quantities of qualitative data can range from physically sorting and storing slips of paper to using one of the several computer software programmes that have been designed to aid in this task. Analysis begins with identification of the themes emerging from the raw data, a process sometimes referred to as "open coding". During open coding, the researcher must identify and tentatively name the conceptual categories into which the phenomena observed will be grouped. The goal is to create descriptive, multidimensional categories which form a preliminary framework for analysis.

Words, phrases or events that appear to be similar can be grouped into the same category. Qualititative research reports are characterised by the use of "voice" in the text; that is, participant quotes that illustrate the themes being described. The next stage of analysis involves re-examination of the categories identified to determine how they are linked, a complex process sometimes called "axial coding". The discrete categories identified in open coding are compared and combined in new ways as the researcher begins to assemble the "big picture."

Researchers and readers share a joint responsibility for establishing the value of the qualitative research product. The following three features of qualitative research should be considered by reviewers:

i) *Coherence*: Does the story make sense? How have the conclusions been supported? To what extent have multiple data sources been used to give credence to the interpretation that has been made?

ii) *Consensus*: The condition in which the readers of a work concur that the findings and/or interpretations reported by the investigator are consistent with their own experience or with the evidence presented.

iii) *Instrumental utility*: The most important test of any qualitative study is its usefulness. A good qualitative study can help to understand a situation that would otherwise be enigmatic or confusing.

## Reliability and Validity in Qualitative Research

Reliability and validity are tools of an essentially positivist epistemology. M. Joppe defines reliability as: "The extent to which results are consistent over time and an accurate representation of the total population under study is referred to as reliability and if the results of a study can be reproduced under a similar methodology, then the research instrument is considered to be reliable".

According to C. Stenbacka, "the concept of reliability is even misleading in qualitative research. If a qualitative study is discussed with reliability as a criterion, the consequence is rather that the study is no good".

To ensure reliability in qualitative research, examination of trustworthiness is crucial. C. Seale, while establishing good quality studies through reliability and validity in qualitative research, states that the "trustworthiness of a research report lies at the heart of issues conventionally discussed as validity and reliability". In contrast, Stenbacka argues that since reliability issue concerns measurements then it has no relevance in qualitative research. She adds the issue of reliability is an irrelevant matter in the judgement of quality of qualitative research. Therefore, if it is used then the "consequence is rather that the study is no good".

The concept of validity is described by a wide range of terms in qualitative studies. This concept is not a single, fixed or universal concept, but "rather a contingent construct, inescapably grounded in the processes and intentions of particular research methodologies and projects". Although some qualitative researchers have argued that the term validity is not applicable to qualitative research, yet at the same time, they have realised the need for some kind of qualifying check or measure for their research.

Many researchers have developed their own concepts of validity and have often generated or adopted what they consider to be more appropriate terms, such as, quality, rigour and trustworthiness. Stenbacka argues that the concept of validity should be redefined for qualitative researches. She describes the notion of reliability as one of the quality concepts in qualitative research which has "to be solved in order to claim a study as part of proper research".

Y. S. Lincoln and E. G. Guba argue that sustaining the trustworthiness of a research report depends on the issues, quantitatively, discussed as validity and reliability. The idea of discovering truth through measures of reliability and validity is replaced by the idea of trustworthiness, which is "defensible" and establishing confidence in the findings. If the issues of reliability, validity, trustworthiness, quality and rigour are meant differentiating a 'good' from 'bad' research then testing and increasing the reliability, validity, trustworthiness, quality and rigour will be important to the research in any paradigm.

Therefore, the quality of a research is related to generalisability of the result and thereby to the testing and increasing the validity or trustworthiness of the research. In contrast, J. A. Maxwell observes that the degree to which an account is believed to be generalisable is a factor that clearly distinguishes quantitative and qualitative research approaches.

In this sense the validity in quantitative research is very specific to the test to which it is applied—where triangulation methods are used in qualitative research. Triangulation is typically a strategy (test) for improving the validity and reliability of research or evaluation of findings. Triangulation has risen an important methodological issue in naturalistic and qualitative approaches to evaluation control bias and establishing valid propositions because traditional scientific techniques are incompatible with this alternate epistemology.

The use of triangulation by stating "triangulation strengthens a study by combining methods. This can mean using several kinds of methods or data, including using both quantitative and qualitative approaches". For example, in using triangulation of several data sources in quantitative research, any exception may lead to a disconfirmation of the hypothesis where exceptions in qualitative research are dealt to modify the theories and are fruitful.

In any qualitative research, the aim is to "engage in research that probes for deeper understanding rather than examining surface features" and constructivism may facilitate toward that aim. The constructivist notion, that reality is changing whether the observer wishes it or not, is an indication of multiple or possibly diverse constructions of reality. Constructivism values multiple realities that people have in their minds.

Therefore, to acquire valid and reliable multiple and diverse realities, multiple methods of searching or gathering data are in order. If this calls for the use of triangulation in the constructivism paradigm, then the use of investigators, method and data triangulations to record the construction of reality is appropriate. An open-ended perspective in constructivism adheres with the notion of data triangulation by allowing participants in a research to assist the researcher in the research question as well as with the data collection.

Engaging multiple methods, such as, observation, interviews and recordings will lead to more valid, reliable and diverse construction of realities. To improve the analysis and understanding of construction of others, triangulation is a step taken by researchers to involve several investigators or peer researchers' interpretation of the data at a different time or location.

## Paradigm Shift of Qualitative Research

In the last decade, qualitative research methods, once considered useful primarily for exploratory purposes in the field of psychology, have gained some acceptance in most scholarly research communities as credible research forms in their own right. The movement has been most evident in the social sciences, education and health care research because qualitative research offers opportunities to understand dimensions of social interactions that traditional research methods do not address. This alternative paradigm provides insights into the why and how dimensions of experience, adding significantly to the completeness of answers provided by research.

Nevertheless, this acceptance has not been without controversy. Fields that have relied heavily on studies based on quantitative measures have been slower to embrace this alternative paradigm. This situation may be based on lack of understanding that the essential purpose of qualitative inquiry is to address different questions and to answer them in different ways. It is not simply a different method, but a completely different paradigm that implies a distinctly different world-view, and a different consideration of the sources of truth. Although some institutions offer alternative tracks in which students may choose between an emphasis in qualitative or quantitative studies, this is not the case in every university.

Since contradictory alternative frameworks are highly resistant to change, students' first exposure to qualitative research may be disruptive as they are faced with positions and definitions that contradict their previous assumptions and expectations about the essential nature of research. It requires a major shift in research paradigm to a perspective that recognises the unique experiences and meaning constructions of individuals as viable subjects for research. If they are to accept the viability of qualitative research, learners may need to break with habits of thought that have become automatic throughout their study of research and recognise that the paradigm they have taken for granted has "as much prescriptive as descriptive power".

Learners strive to maintain coherence and consistency in their theories in order to construct viable intellectual frameworks that are more powerful than existing perspectives. There are six positions learners may choose to take as an alternative to conceptual change. These positions, derived from numerous studies, range from simply ignoring the information to accommodation of peripheral change in ways that force only minor modifications on an existing conceptual system or theory.

Three major dimensions influence whether or not learners are willing to change their theories to accept new information. The nature of the existing theory is critical, particularly in its level of entrenchment, in the ontological belief systems that support it, in the epistemological commitments aligned with them, and in the related knowledge that depends on these theories. The new theory must be characterised by plausibility and quality, and the data that supports the new theory must be credible, unambiguous, and the evidence of it occur frequently enough to be convincing.

Learners also must be willing to consider the new theory through deep rather than superficial processing strategies. The usefulness of the new theory and learners' personal and professional interests play important roles in either supporting or undermining possible conceptual shifts. The system of beliefs typically held by students trained in the quantitative paradigm may or may not be based on an articulated understanding of the nature of knowledge and of how we come to know. They approach a class in qualitative research methods with a conceptual framework—a theory that organises these beliefs. Their commitments to the quantitative perspective may involve epistemic and motivational dimensions as well as cognitive ones.

Many of these connections are contradicted by their encounter with qualitative assumptions and methods. Entrenchment of their prior definitions of research, the professional context that supports a quantitative ecology and ontological and epistemological beliefs that can be inferred from their existing theories of research can make the assumptions of the qualitative perspectives difficult to accept. The inherent ambiguity of much of qualitative methodology, which is by nature fluid and interpretive, can also make this approach to research unconvincing to one who holds a well integrated prior theory.

Conceptual change research also explains why the qualitative paradigm would be particularly attractive to some individuals. Although they may have had long-term exposure to, and work within, the quantitative paradigm, the beliefs these people hold about research may not be deeply connected to other dimensions of themselves as persons and professionals. Exposure and knowledge do not necessarily result in closely held beliefs or well-integrated, useful, perspectives. It is possible that the traditional approach to research has not been incorporated into their ontological and epistemological belief systems. They may not have meaningful connections to the research perspectives they have been taught because the precision of positivist methodology does not fit well with the emerging psychology of learning evidenced in a variety of fields, including psychology, cognition, and counselling.

Some researchers and teachers prefer to minimise specific methodological approaches within qualitative research in favour of a general qualitative method. This approach helped them recognise the questions implied by different kinds of qualitative inquiry.

## References

Christensen, D. H., "The Use of Qualitative Methods in Family and Consumer Sciences: A Reflection", *Family and Consumer Sciences Research Journal 27*, no. 4, June 1999.

Creswell, J. W., *Qualitative Inquiry and Re-search Design: Choosing among Five Traditions*, Thousand Oaks, CA: Sage, 1998.

Eisner, E., *The Enlightened Eye: Qualitative Inquiry and the Enhancement of Educa-tional Practice*, New York: Macmillan, 1991.

Garman, N., "Qualitative Inquiry: Meaning and Menace for Educational Researchers", In *Qualitative Research Practice in Adult Education*, edited by P. Willis and B. Neville, pp. 11-29. Ringwood, Victoria, Australia: David Lovell Publishing, 1996.

Golafshani, Nahid, Understanding Reliability and Validity in Qualitative Research, *The Qualitative Report,* University of

Toronto, Toronto, Ontario, Canada, Volume 8, Number 4 December 2003.

Gregson, J. A., "Editorial: Reflecting on Qualitative Research and Vocational Education", *Journal of Vocational Education Research 23*, no. 4 (1998): 265-270.

Hoepfl, M. C., "Choosing Qualitative Research: A Primer for Technology Education Researchers", *ln Journal of Technology Education 9*, no. 1: 47-63, 1997

Reisetter, Marcia, Melinda Yexley, Deborah Bonds, Holly Nikels, William McHenry, "Shifting Paradigms and Mapping the Process: Graduate Students Respond to Qualitative Research", *The Qualitative Report,* Volume 8, Number 3, September 2003.

# 2

# Teaching as a Moral Activity

Teaching and research activities are separate and distinct and are not to be confused. However, research is a strong condition for teaching: being engaged in research of a frame-developing kind and projecting that research to wider publics is a strong—although not exactly necessary and certainly not sufficient—condition of teaching that is aimed at about bringing supercomplexity in the minds of students. If this perspective is accepted, there are major implications for how teachers teach and students are assessed.

Powerful factors influencing how students perceived the relation between staff research and their own learning were their own motivation, their year or level of study and academic discipline. Students who claimed to be interested in learning for its own sake were more likely to express positive attitudes to academic research and staff involvement in that research.

Young people are part of a rapidly changing knowledge society where they will need sound general education, good communication skills, flexibility and adaptability to continue their learning throughout their lives. Many students leaving schools now face a world where much of the work they will do has not yet been imagined. Individuals will need the capacity to continually reinvent themselves, as will organisations.

The ability to access and generate new knowledge in a purposeful fashion, and the need to move beyond content to critical analysis and an understanding of emerging trends and issues, places great demands on our education and training systems to deliver not simply specific skills and knowledge, but also the attitudes and aptitudes to sustain learning throughout life.

Developing and improving the scientific literacy of students is a fundamental role of school science education for all students, and a priority at this time is to consolidate and improve the quality of school science. Making science more relevant for all young people may help increase the number who choose to take science further. Declining enrolments in physics and chemistry in the final years of schooling is of concern, especially in the way it may reduce subsequent options for students.

Technology education is important in this regard, for it needs to create skilled, creative and flexible young people who can apply their learnings in a dynamic and ever-changing information economy and knowledge-based society. Equally so, the application of information and communication technologies (ICT) has a wide impact on schools and learning because it provides alternate sources of information and scope for new approaches to student learning that may place additional pressures on the roles of teachers and schools to meet student and parental expectations.

The development of a culture of innovation in schools cannot be confined to the teaching and learning of science, technology and mathematics. The creation of school environments where students develop capacities to generate new and innovative ideas is an issue for all teachers, not just those charged specifically with fostering scientific, technological and mathematical skills. In this context, it is important to create understanding in young people that science, technology and mathematics are not in themselves isolated areas of study, and that they interrelate within a broad context of learnings.

Quality teaching and learning are important for teachers and students across the schools. Society would cope with change in a more purposeful and cohesive fashion if all are supported to attain the necessary literacy and numeracy skills that provide the foundations for developing more complex analytical, conceptual and communication skills—skills which sustain public discourse and reasoned public policy development. A broad education base which develops attitudes that support continual learning supports a more cohesive and more personally satisfying society.

The role of the teacher is progressively being broadened from that of the expert who imparts knowledge to one that includes mentor or guide—one who extends students' deep understandings and facilitates the acquisition of higher order thinking skills and creative problem solving skills—skills that are critical for the development of an innovative culture for tomorrow.

The demand for teachers comprises two key elements: the 'New' demand arising from population and economic growth; and the 'Replacement' demand arising from the need to replace existing teachers who resign, retire or leave their profession for other reasons. This demand for teachers is created by existing and new permanent positions in the public and private school systems as well as short-term vacancies. The latter meets teacher labour market demands through the provision of contractual short-term supplies of teachers to meet rapidly emerging needs, or to provide teaching resources where holders of permanent positions are on long or short-term leave.

For instance, teachers of vocational education and training in schools also work in the vocational education and training system. The supply of teachers to meet demand is derived from people with teaching qualifications currently not working as teachers, new entrants to the profession who have completed teaching qualifications, and the migration of people with teaching qualifications.

There is some flexibility and autonomy at the school level in some areas for principals to directly employ recent teacher graduates in government schools. However, there is little flexibility when it comes to ongoing professional development of teachers once employed, and evidence suggests that there is little support or non-monetary reward for those teachers who initiate their own further professional development.

As a result, the values and benefits of being part of the teaching profession beyond remuneration through salary may not be widely understood. In addition, it is likely that some teaching conditions – such as non-teaching responsibilities, teaching in rural and remote locations, insufficient cross-jurisdictional portability of qualifications and experience, perceived lack of professional, administrative and personal support, and recognition for ongoing professional learning – may be disincentives for qualified persons to seek teacher employment.

Universities play a critical role in facilitating the entry of potential teachers into the profession. A number of universities are offering or developing innovative approaches to pre-service teacher education, and some are now conducting outreach programmes from their science/ mathematics faculties which target school leavers. These programmes involve university students and staff visiting schools to assist teachers in the delivery of the science, technology and mathematics curriculum and to encourage students to continue to study science at the tertiary level.

There are traditional and alternative pathways into the teaching profession. Traditional pathways for intending teachers may involve a direct transition from school to undergraduate teacher education, or a postgraduate teacher education award following a first degree. Education authorities provide some programmes to retrain teachers to teach those specialist areas in demand and also provide some support for teachers in these areas to upgrade their level of qualification.

As learning organisations, schools are increasingly reaching into the broader community, from where they can build links and partnerships, and draw resources and expertise. This is particularly evident in school–industry-community partnerships which support vocational learning, enterprise and career education, and transitions through and from school. These arrangements create and foster active relationships between the community, business and schools to enable a learning environment of continuous exposure to ideas and innovation.

Both principal-leaders and teacher-leaders are important for successful in-school innovation. There is potential for effective school leadership through mentoring of teachers and student teachers to create a climate for effective teaching based on the development of an innovative culture. In many instances teachers are identified as role models for students. There are also arguments that the teaching population should reflect the diversity of the wider community.

Ideally, technological tools should be a seamless part of the school environment, requiring no more prior learning to apply than, say, electricity. Teachers and students would use technological tools—or not—in learning situations, depending on whether they helped one to learn in that context. School administrative records and cafeteria food requirements would be updated automatically from entry-screening systems, or perhaps the attendance software on a teacher's personal digital assistant (PDA).

But the technological tools available do not fit together this seamlessly yet, and teachers and staff (and students) need training and professional development in order to make the best use of technology in schools. In fact, providing sufficient development and training to give staff skills and confidence in the use of technology is widely viewed as an ongoing challenge to schools. Technology use also has to be taught in the context of educational or management activities, which means that measuring the extent of "pure" technology preparation is very difficult.

The term professional development is used to represent learning activities of all kinds for school staff that prepare them to use technology in the school setting. The following are the learning activities in professional development:

i) familiarisation with the operation of equipment and software;
ii) development of proficiency in the use of the technology "tools" to carry out school tasks;
iii) the application of software and applications to the management of school activities, whether instructional or administrative; and

iv) the integration of technology into teaching, learning, and administrative processes.

Professional development, is explicitly understood to extend to administrative and support staff whose jobs have changed and will continue to change due to the infusion of technology in schools. Professional development includes support for teachers and staff as they apply technology to their evolving practices, from lesson plans and curriculum integration to record keeping and administrative functions. It is an ongoing process that cannot be satisfied with one-time training in a particular technology.

The methods and content of technology-related professional development are changing as quickly as technology itself. Technology has brought a windfall for delivery methods in professional development. Online delivery means can help educators to find the best time for training based on their own schedules. Video and audio conferencing allow teachers access to both instructional and collegial support. E-mail and e-bulletin boards enable teachers to share information and solve problems. Still, taken as a whole, technology cannot solve the problem of allocating the time needed for ongoing professional development to establish and maintain proficiency in technology use.

Tailoring evaluation methods to professional development programmes makes sense—data on how teachers and administrators progress and how they are using new technologies to promote student achievement give great insight into what technology is doing for schools. By evaluating professional development, technology planners and administrators can learn what is working, and what or who needs help.

## Effective Measures of Teaching and Research

Both teaching and research are highly complex activities and both are notoriously difficult to measure; yet the measures reveal an instrumental conception of both activities. The implied relationship between teaching and research will be a function of the measures used in the correlations—what data were available and how they were gathered. These different methods of data collection and the underlying assumptions become particularly problematic when the data are aggregated and studies synthesised to produce supposedly superior and more powerful findings.

C.L. Colbeck found that teaching and research activities can overlap but in very specific ways. For example, research is much more likely to overlap with independent project work or dissertation supervision than it is with classroom teaching. In order to carry out statistical analyses, good teaching and research are defined by the measures used to assess them—such as numbers of publications, citation scores, judgements of departmental heads or peers and research grants in the case of research; and student and staff ratings of teaching effectiveness.

Research productivity is frequently confused with both quality and impact. That measures of research productivity reflected through citation counts come the closest to measuring research quality. The use and interpretation of citation counts varies according to discipline and poses difficulties in comparing data across disciplines. If the view of research productivity is largely mechanistic, so too is that of teaching. Yet good teaching implies detailed subject knowledge which can be communicated and transformed in different situations and ways of responding to these situations. Complementary to this are the developments in learning theory.

Contemporary views of effective tertiary teaching for learning have moved well beyond direct transmission models. The concept of effective student learning, or deep learning, encompasses a range of ways in which students engage in enquiry. It situates knowledge in relation both to what students know and how the knowledge is to be applied. It encourages responsibility and autonomy.

Critics of American undergraduate higher education such as Clark and Boyer hold that research and teaching conflict and that undergraduate education suffers as a result. Boyer asserts that research activity competes with teaching obligations for time and content. To accommodate research activity, teaching loads are reduced, teaching assistants are assigned to teaching large classes, and students needs are ignored because staff pursue their own scholarly interests. Studies conducted with British and Australian undergraduate students suggest that students from a range of disciplines perceive clear benefits from staff research including staff enthusiasm and the credibility of staff and the institution.

It is necessary reassess and redefine the roles of teachers and students in the development of a culture of critical enquiry in higher education. An unknown future faces the academic profession at the beginning of the twenty-first century. In the face of shaky financial underpinnings, shifting curricular priorities, unpredictable social needs, crises of public confidence and the revolution in electronic resources, academics and administrators are rethinking patterns of work and institutional organisation to maintain the scholarly environments that have traditionally defined universities.

A number of government-led initiatives throughout the 1980s and 1990s becoming less insular and introverted in their activities and more accountable for the ways in which their academic activities met public expectations. Internal and external quality exercises have revealed that universities are increasingly responsive to students and the wider community. 'as far as core activities are concerned, conscientious attention to teaching is more widespread, and efforts to meet community needs and international standards in research have become generally better informed and more professional.

The introduction of performance-based funding measures for research has had considerable impact upon research output. The measures have also highlighted anomalies brought about by the increasing scholarly diversity in universities. One motivation for extending concepts of scholarship is linked to identifying how to appropriately recognise, value and reward the diversity of academic work. From this perspective definitions of scholarship that embrace and integrate teaching and research better reflect endeavours within the modern university. While institutional mission statements increasingly refer to relationships between teaching and research, issues at the very heart of current practice must be addressed before staff efforts can gain appropriate reward.

One of the most talked-about issues in higher education has been the system of rewards and incentives in universities. As a consequence the balance between teaching and research has been rethought and revised. But this has been largely because of a focus on teaching and learning. The best teaching occurs when active researchers use their expertise to inform teaching, while research ideas and approaches are stimulated and sharpened through interactions with students.

## References

Atin, A. W. and Chang, M. J., "Colleges that emphasise research and reaching, can you have your cake and eat it too?", *Change*, pp. 45- 49, 1995.

Bakker, G., "Using 'pedagogical-impact statements' to make teaching and research symbiotic activities", *Chronicle of Higher Education*, 17 March, p. B3, 1995.

Barnett, R., "Linking teaching and research, a critical inquiry", *Journal of Higher Education*, 63(6), pp. 619- 636, 1992.

Batty, M., and Mathews, S. A., "Relationship between teaching and research?", *Area*, 20, pp. 158-162, 1988.

Brew, A., "Research and teaching: changing relationships in a changing context", *Studies in Higher Education*, 24(3), pp. 291-391, 1999.

Clark, B.R., "The modern integratio n of research activities with teaching and learning", *Journal of Higher Education*, 68(3), pp. 242- 255, 1997.

Downes, Toni, Andrew Fluck, Pam Gibbons, Ralph Leonard, Caroline Matthews, Ron Oliver, Margaret Vickers and Michelle Williams, *Making Better Connections:Models of teacher professional development for the integration of information and communication technology into classroom practice*, Department of Education,Training and Youth Affairs, Canberra, 2001.

Elton, L., *Research and teaching: what are the real relationships?* (forthcoming)", 1999.

Foote, K.E., "Bringing faculty on-line; inspiring and sustaining innovation in information and computer technologies (ICT)", *Journal of Geography in Higher Education*, 23(1), pp. 5- 8, 1999.

Jenkins, Alan, *The Relationship Between Teaching and Research: where does geography stand and deliver*, Oxfor University, UK, Journal of Geography in Higher Education, Vol. 24. No. 3, 2000

Knight, P.G., "The relationship between teaching and research", Area, 19, pp. 350-352, 1987.

Ramsey, Gregor, *Quality Matters—Revitalising Teaching: Critical Times, Critical Choices*, News South Wales Department of Education and Training, Sydney, 2000.

# 3

# Classroom Assessments in Teaching and Learning

The process in education that most directly connects with student learning is teaching. If the educational community hopes to take the next step in improving students' learning, it must analyse and improve classroom teaching. Without attention to teaching, all of the reform efforts will soon hit a premature ceiling. Student performance might rise on some assessments, but the gains will be relatively narrow. All good ideas implemented outside the classroom, such as more focused and coherent curricula, reach students only through the way in which teacher and students interact about the subject. Teaching is the key to further improvement.

Some teachers do create their own innovative methods but the way most teachers and students interact during classroom lessons has not changed much during the twentieth century. This suggests that teaching is a cultural activity. Being a cultural activity, teaching is not learned by sitting through courses, reading documents, and taking exams. It is learned through participating in the cultures of schools, as students and then as teachers. This means that teaching will improve only when the cultures of schools change so that they become places where teachers, not just students, learn.

Most US schools are not structured as places for teachers to learn but this is exactly the kind of culture that is reported in schools that witness continuing improvements in classroom practice. The classroom walls that separate teachers begin to dissolve and teachers begin observing each other teach and talking with each other about teaching. They focus on problems of their own practice, and their conversations are filled with references to their students' thinking and to the directions in which the curriculum can lead students' thinking. They try new approaches, monitor the effects, and reflect on the successes and failures. In brief, teaching improves in schools that metamorphose into cultures of collegiality and experimentation.

For example, most elementary and middle school Japanese teachers engage in a process they call lesson study or lesson research. Japanese teachers form small study groups for the school year organised around grade levels and/or subject areas. One group might be five 3rd and 4th-grade teachers focusing on mathematics. Often, the group's goal is to re-design a few lessons to better achieve the goal of the school for the year and to improve students' learning of a particular topic.

A striking feature of the lesson plans is a prediction of the different responses that students are likely to give to each of the tasks presented in the lesson and suggestions for how teachers can use these responses in a class discussion. What makes lesson study an intriguing model for improving teaching in the US is that it is sensitive to the complex, cultural nature of teaching and it is consistent with the principles, noted earlier, that typify successful efforts in American schools. In addition, lesson study has several important features that can amplify the effectiveness of current programmes and launch new ones.

i) With its focus on planning and testing lessons, lesson study sets a concrete well-defined task for the collaborative work of teachers.

ii) Since lessons provide the forum for student learning, lesson study must attend to all important features of teaching and how they interact.

iii) The process of lesson study conceives of teacher development as an outcome of improving teaching, rather than vice versa. By improving a few lessons with great care, teachers build their own capacity to teach all lessons more effectively.

iv) Lesson study is not limited to a particular subject or method of teaching; as long as the student learning goals are clear, the lessons that most effectively help students achieve them will survive.

v) Lessons are the currency of teaching, so lesson study enables teachers to record and share their successful ideas in ways that are useful for other teachers and thus spreads improvements across classrooms, schools, and districts.

vi) Lesson study affords scaling up, both in the accumulation of effective lessons and in reaching across geographic boundaries of districts and states.

American educators, policy makers, and politicians have a tradition of ruining good ideas for improving teaching and learning in schools. Most often, the abuse comes as ideas are oversimplified and sold as quick fixes. Quick fixes might affect the margins of classroom practice but they do not penetrate its core. Americans are extremely impatient and want reforms rather than improvements. The consequence of rushing to reform is the absence of lasting improvement. The pendulum swings but core classroom practices remain pretty much the same. Changing teaching methods in the United States, and changing the way in which teachers learn to teach, are changes in culture.

## Principles of Teaching and Learning

The following are the seven principles for good practice in undergraduate education which guide teaching and learning in the school being evaluated:

i) Good practice encourages student-faculty contact

ii) Good practice encourages cooperation among students

iii) Good practice encourages active learning

iv) Good practice gives prompt feedback

v) Good practice emphasises time on task
vi) Good practice communicates high expectations
vii) Good practice respects diverse talents and ways of learning

*Good practice encourages student-faculty contact*: Frequent student-faculty contact in and out of classes is the most important factor in student motivation and involvement. Faculty concern helps students get through rough times and keep on working.

Email was the primary form of private communication between instructor and students. Three out of four of the instructors were good at encouraging contact through private email messages. All of the instructors went out of their way to make it clear to students that they could be contacted via email and telephone. A couple of the instructors also invited students to have unscheduled face-to-face meetings with them in order to help students who were struggling with the learning experience done entirely at a distance over the internet. Listservs and class bulletin boards were the main source of public communication between instructors and students.

With a few notable exceptions, instructors were respectful in the ways that they responded to students publicly. There was at least one instance where an instructor publicly confronted a student in a way that the evaluators felt should have been saved for a private dialogue between instructor and student. Building trust with the students enhances student-faculty communication. All of the instructors to one degree or another built trust with their students by providing opportunities for strengthening their relationship. This was done by sharing values, attitudes, and experiences with the students and encouraging them to do the same.

While instructors were good at encouraging email contact, none of the instructors clearly and adequately communicated their email response policies to the students. This is an important step in establishing student faculty contact. The 24-hour availability of email to the students provides a mechanism for contacting faculty unparalleled in the past. Students often assume that instructors have easy, constant access to their email. If they contact an instructor and don't hear back within an expected timeframe they may feel that the instructor is ignoring their request. This kind of misunderstanding can be reduced if the instructor communicates to the students a general policy or timeline for answering student's email questions.

In the class that used a listserv, the instructor claimed that she periodically contacted students she hadn't heard from in a while. There was no clear indication beyond that of how well she kept track of who was on task and who was falling through the cracks. The job of keeping track of students' progress in this class was difficult because the majority of the assignments were due all at once in a final portfolio at the end of the course. Thus there was no clear checkpoint for determining if a student was on track.

*Good practice encourages cooperation among students*: Good learning, like good work, is collaborative and social, not competitive and isolated. Working with others often increases involvement in learning. Sharing one's own ideas and responding to others' reactions improves thinking and deepens understanding. One way that instructors have encouraged cooperation among students is by including group projects and assignments as a part of the course. Most instructors include some kind of "ice breaker" at the beginning of the course. These are good for helping the distance students get to know each other better.

Create activities and assignments that foster a sense of community among the students. It can be much more difficult for students at a distance to gain a sense of belonging or community with each other. One course had virtually no meaningful student-student contact during the semester while the other three classes had varying degrees of student-student contact. The courses could begin with a structured activity in which students are asked to share and find out about each other's interests. Peer interaction was a weak part of most of the courses.

Instructors should develop assignments that require meaningful peer interaction. Peer interaction will help to enrich the learning experience for the students as well as take the responsibility off the instructor for being the only feedback provider. Students might take the leading role in class discussions. For example, a group of students might lead the discussion by coming up with a set of questions while another group summarises the discussion at the end.

Develop a mechanism for evaluating individual participation and contribution to group projects. If there is a collaborative project as part of the course, it is important that a mechanism be incorporated to encourage individual accountability and responsibility. Determining the level of individual contribution can typically be done through the process of peer and self-evaluations. In these evaluations students who worked with each other on a team are asked to evaluate peer contributions to the team effort.

*Good practice encourages active learning*: Overall, the instructors in all of the courses that were evaluated did a very good job of encouraging students to engage in active learning. They were particularly good at getting students to relate the ideas that they were learning to real-world issues. This was often done by getting students to do real-world projects or authentic assignments. While reading was usually required, assignments were often structured to get the students to do something with that knowledge rather than just regurgitating it.

*Good practice gives prompt feedback*: In classes, students need frequent opportunities to perform and receive feedback on their performance. At various points during college, and at its end, students need chances to reflect on what they have learned, what they still need to know, and how they might assess themselves. There are typically two main types of feedback:

i) acknowledgment feedback
ii) information feedback

Acknowledgment feedback is feedback that confirms or assures the student that some event has taken place. In a face-to-face environment this kind of feedback happens all the time and is often communicated through nonverbal cues. For example, when a student raises her hand to ask a question in class, she knows that the instructor has seen her request because of the eye contact she makes with the instructor. Similarly when a student submits an assignment in class, he gets visual confirmation that the instructor has received the assignment when the instructor picks up the stack of assignments and puts it into a briefcase at the end of class. This kind of feedback is often not readily available to students in an online learning environment.

Information Feedback is feedback that is informational or evaluative in nature. It is often manifested as the answer to a student question or as an assignment grade and comments. This type of feedback is typically explicitly given in both face-to-face and online environments. With the exception of one course, the instructors were good about giving information feedback on assignments and projects in a timely manner. The turnaround time for giving feedback on assignments in all cases, however, could be improved. A good goal to shoot for is a turnaround time of one week or less. When instructors set student expectations by communicating a clear feedback response policy it reduces student stress.

While all instructors but one were good at giving informational feedback, improvements could be made in providing more and better acknowledgment feedback. Instructors can alleviate student concerns by sending them a brief note of acknowledgment when they receive an assignment via email. Also, if an instructor is too busy, for some reason, to give a detailed answer to a student question in a timely manner, the instructor should give the student an acknowledgment email stating that they have received the question and will address the question later when they have more time. All feedback does not and should not necessarily come from the instructors. Assignments and projects should be structured so that students can provide feedback to each other on them. Instructors need not become overwhelmed by the amount of feedback to give the students if they are properly leveraging the capabilities of other students in the class.

*Good practice emphasises time on task*: Learning to use one's time well is critical for students and professionals alike. Students need help in learning effective time management. Allocating realistic amounts of time means effective learning for students and effective teaching for faculty. Among assignments, some tasks require much more time than others. Most courses had assignments with specific deadlines that required students to participate in the class on a regular basis.

Overall instructors did a good job of underscoring the importance of regular work, steady application, sound self-pacing, and scheduling. This can be communicated explicitly through email, etc., as well as through the structuring and due dates of the assignments. Asynchronous conferencing can be a good way to improve student time on task. If the course assignments need some campus-based resources (e.g., CDs, videos, books) instructors should try to make arrangement with the related university department for the students' to easily access the resources.

Good practice communicates high expectations. High expectations are important for everyone—for the poorly prepared, for those unwilling to exert themselves, and for the bright and well motivated. Expecting students to perform well becomes a self-fulfilling prophecy when teachers and institutions hold high expectations for themselves and make extra efforts. Instructors were good at publicly calling attention to excellent performance by the students. Instructors did a good job of balancing the praise given with the advice offered to the students.

Good practice respects diverse talents and ways of learning: People bring different talents and styles of learning to college. Students need the opportunity to show their talents and learn in ways that work for them. Then they can be pushed to learning in new ways that do not come easily. All of the instructors were conscientious about trying to incorporate diverse viewpoints and methods of learning into their courses. The instructors for the courses that were evaluated used many different methods to bring diverse talents and ways of learning into the course. One method used was to allow students to shape their own coursework by choosing project topics.

Instructors also attempted to learn about the different backgrounds and interests of the students through online icebreaker activities at the beginning of the semester. Instructors also were good about encouraging students to express their diverse points of view. Additionally instructors often included learning exercises filled with real-life examples that represented diverse, unique perspectives.

## Research Capacity of Teaching and Learning

Teaching and learning activities are endemic and important aspects of human life, and especially of life in today's societies, that they are properly the subject of research within several of the social science disciplines. It has been persuasively argued, furthermore, that one of the major limitations of educational research generally, and of research on teaching and learning in particular, is the limited extent to which it tends to be informed by relevant theoretical work in the social sciences.

From such perspectives, any research into teaching and learning that is designed to be of practical use is likely to be seen as 'applied' or at best 'strategic'; and it is no doubt because of this, and because of the low status of applied research, that so little research is done in education by mainstream social scientists. The contrast between educational research, concerned as it generally is with implications for policy and practice, and disciplined-based research in the social sciences is a sharp one.

Within the field of educational research, there is a widespread assumption that the value of research must in large measure be judged in terms of its usefulness in informing policy and practice. Thus virtually all educational research is 'applied' or at least 'strategic', although few educational researchers would find these categories helpful or appropriate. There remain, however, important distinctions to be made between ways in which educational research into teaching and learning might be useful, and significant controversies about the value, feasibility and appropriateness of these.

There is little doubt that research does influence teaching and learning in such ways, although the indirectness and the timescales involved makes quantification of such influence and of consequent benefits virtually impossible. Research undertaken with this view of its usefulness has in recent years been predominantly qualitative in nature, although quantitative research can serve the same kind of function. Capacity for research of this kind is likely to be of a generally academic and social scientific kind. Capacity for its use will depend on the general interpenetration of the academic educational world with that of policy and practice.

Teachers should have access to evidence from controlled studies about the procedures most likely to achieve specific desired learning outcomes in specified types of circumstances. The relative scarcity of such research must to some extent be because of the difficulty of doing it with a persuasive degree of validity, a difficulty which is due in part to the technically demanding quantitative research involved and in part to the organisational problems of achieving the willing collaboration of groups of schools, teachers, students, parents and/or learners in non-institutional contexts.

Educational research into teaching and learning emphasise the theoretical or generalisable knowledge sought by professional academic researchers, other approaches place more emphasis on the local context and on the role of practitioners. Long-established theoretical perspectives emphasising investigation aimed at understanding or 'evaluation' of specific local institutions or cases rather than the aspiration to generalise, and the importance of the 'teacher as researcher', ideally placed to engage in action research on his or her own practice, combine here with more recent concerns that schools can and should themselves be 'knowledge-creating'.

Such an emphasis on teachers and schools as the agents of research, and of specific institutions or local contexts tas the primary beneficiaries, implies some merging or at least some redefinition of the roles of schools and of academic researchers. It does not imply any diminution in the need for rigour in research on teaching and learning, but it does suggest the critical importance of partnerships between researching schools and academic research institutions. A rather different tradition is that of developmental research, concerned to produce new curricula or teaching approaches, in which schools work closely with development agencies.

Such developmental research was very significant in the UK in the seventies and remains of importance in continental Europe and the United States. Today, capacity for such developmental research would depend on strong knowledge-creating schools working in dialogue with external developmental agencies. Just as teaching and learning are activities widely pursued outside educational institutions, so research into such teaching and learning probably occurs in other organisational contexts most obviously in relation to industrial training.

Schools are not the only organisation in which capacity for research into teaching and learning may be needed and may exist. Finally, it is important to include a less ambitious but none the less radical and challenging conception of how schools, and teachers and learners in other contexts, might be engaged with research. Contributing to research-based knowledge is not an aspiration which all educational institutions, teachers and learners will share. On the other hand, if research is to be seen as useful for learning and teaching, then a basic aspiration of researchers in this field must be that the learning teacher, the learning learner and especially the learning school will be learning from, among other things, research.

'Capacity', in its literal meaning, is concerned with how much can be put into a space or a container. It is a quantitative concept, and it is concerned with potential. 'Research capacity' is not then concerned with how much research is being done, but with how much could be done.

'Potential' might however imply what could be possible in the future; and presumably, with time and investment and sufficient inducement, millions of people and thousands of organisations could eventually become effectively geared to engage in research on teaching and learning.

Motivation would include the extent to which research in general, and specific kinds of research into teaching and learning in particular, were priority concerns within the cultures within which the people work or recognised obligations of the roles in which people are employed, and also the established common incentives, for individuals and institutions, financial and of other kinds, which lead people to engage, or not to engage, in these kinds of research. Opportunity is the most complex of these three general factors. Most basically, it includes people's working conditions, such as whether or not people have the necessary time, facilities and support services to make research of the relevant kinds possible.

However, in considering research capacity as a general concept one further consideration is necessary. Whichever approach to research on teaching and learning one might consider, there is no doubt that doing such research well is a highly complex and difficult task; and while there might, under attractive conditions, be many people willing to do such research, and able to bring some relevant expertise to it, estimates of capacity will vary depending on the standards one sets for expertise, and more generally for the quality of the research that could be done.

The capacity for applied social science research into teaching and learning takes as its starting point theories relating to teaching or learning within one or more of the social science disciplines, and which explores the implications of these theories for teaching and learning in particular contexts, with a view to informing policy or practice. Such a purpose implies that there should be a concern with understanding good or effective practice, or with optimising such desirable practice.

Conceptualisation research would include, most obviously, a thorough understanding of the relevant theoretical area. It would also include a good wide-ranging social scientific methodological expertise, of quantitative and qualitative kinds, including extensive skills in assessing educational attainments. Finally, it would include an understanding of the cultural and organisational constraints and priorities operating in the context with which the research was concerned. Motivation to engage in this kind of research would depend on attributing importance, for whatever reason, to generation of the distinctively applied kind of knowledge with which such research is concerned. It seems clear that the combination of motivation with expertise is critical to the country's capacity for this kind of research into teaching and learning.

Within social scientific academic fields, status, promotion and access to research funding through peer review all appear to be strongly associated with actual or potential contributions to the core theoretical disciplines, and those who identify with these academic communities therefore tend to be extrinsically (and also no doubt intrinsically, having chosen to enter these fields) motivated to direct their research efforts towards such basic research. Motivation to engage in applied research (into teaching and learning, for example) is therefore rare.

Opportunity to do research of this kind depends first on how far doing research of any kind is part of, is facilitated by, or is at least a realistic possibility in relation to, one's terms of employment. Second, the opportunity might depend on being specifically employed to do research of this kind or on having some degree of freedom to choose the nature of the research one will do. Third, opportunity may be enhanced or restricted by whether or not one has, or can readily establish, close working relationships with institutions or groups engaged in the teaching and learning one might wish to investigate.

Academic social scientists who might be more motivated to engage in applied research into teaching and learning, and might also have superior institutional facilities for doing so, could be found in university education departments, although there might be relatively few of these. A third context in which social scientists with relevant expertise might be found, is in independent research organisations. Motivation for this kind of research in these organisations is likely to depend, even more heavily than in university departments, on external financial incentives; and good opportunities for this kind of research would depend on these external incentives being sufficiently sustained to justify the development of close working relationships with institutions or groups engaged in teaching and learning.

The contribution of the research improved understanding of knowledge and skills, and especially to the processes involved in the acquisition of knowledge and skills for their effective use, is quite disappointing. Many of the limitations seem to be associated with a major gap that is apparent between the two academic subject areas which might reasonably be expected to generate such understanding through their research, education and psychology. That gap is multidimensional, and stretches across just those areas where research is most needed.

Thus even the extensive research reported on the cognition of pre-school children, and of adults, seems of very little relevance to the practically important issues about the learning of knowledge and skills, and the facilitation of that learning, which concern not only educators but also parents, employers and those seeking employment, autonomy, understanding and effective engagement as citizens in a modern society. These are of course educational issues, and one might therefore look to research in education to confront them.

Educational research seems to be very narrowly focused on educational institutions and within educational ideologies. The Teaching and Learning Research Programme has a distinctive opportunity to:

i) promote exemplary collaborative research between university education and social science departments; and in so doing to
ii) expand high-quality capacity for research into teaching and learning by recruiting social scientists to work in this area; and

iii) develop high-quality capacity for research into teaching and learning by persuading and enabling educational researchers to become more knowledgeable about relevant social science theory and more expert in using it in their research.

The position of teachers in the school was thought to have a bearing on research capacity building for teaching and learning. Some had travelled through the system at a time when the culture was different. Some others when promoted to management positions tended to become less interested in classroom processes and more interested in management and administrative activities. Facilitating infrastructures for research capacity building in schools were thought to include:

i) fostering a culture of continuing professional development;
ii) building into the school timetable time for collaborative research;
iii) negotiating formal and sustained links with HEIs;
iv) full-time employment of a professional researcher to act as a mentor, a facilitator and a coach;
v) accredited in-house in-service arrangements with research components;
vi) clear expectations about how teachers will spend non-teaching time;
vii) cultivating a language of research.

The greatest benefits to research capacity building in teaching and learning contexts was where people's research led to more generalised understandings and where teachers worked with more experienced researchers to determine the implications of their research, or the research of others, for classroom practices.

Most research into teaching and/or learning is likely to be conducted in university departments of education; and most of it is likely to be aimed at developing understanding of teaching and learning, rather than being aimed at providing directly applicable findings about effective methods of teaching and learning.

How can we be teaching if students are not learning, as the old saying goes? The answer is simple: Some students are ready for the curriculum; others are not. Unfortunately, the typical professor cannot design the perfect lesson that will bridge the gap among the students in class, and cannot construct or buy the perfect test that will show the differences. Therefore, if it is all up to them, higher education must admit defeat. This new change in emphasis of the education model is reflected in several areas. The first area concerns the central focus of education. Rather than the traditional teacher-centered model, the focus shifts to being learning-centred. Instead of the focusing on the broadcaster of information, it is now on effectiveness of the transmission process.

The traditional instructional model encourages an increase in the quantity of information that is presented to students and use of new instructional technologies to transmit it. After a long period of focusing energies and committing scarce resources to improving teaching, many bruised and battered educators are turning their attention to improving the efficiency and effectiveness of the learning environment. Rather than examining how much information was delivered, the question is how much does the student understand. This new emphasis embraces the appropriate use of state-of-the-art technology to enhance instruction delivery.

But not to the extent that students are overwhelmed with content without a corresponding learning environment that insures mastery learning. Another dimension of the new education model regards measuring the effectiveness of education. The traditional periodic major examinations, although perhaps effective in assessing the degree to which students have copied a field of data, are insufficient measures of this level of learning. The new model uses continuous classroom assessment through both formal and informal means to provide feedback to both the students and the instructors concerning the effectiveness of the learning.

Students are more complicated that television sets that receive programmes from the broadcasters. If the first dimension recognises that professors cannot deliver the perfect lecture and the second recognises that there is no perfect test, the next dimension of the new model is more personal. The first two dimensions tell us that we must change what we do. The third tells us we must recognise who our students are and we must change the way we think about ourselves and our students. The changes are more than demographic. They include that the gender balance is shifting and that the mean age is rising.

Traditional aged students come from secondary education where collaborative learning activities have accustomed students to working in small groups and engaging in peer discussions regarding course material. Although previous generations of students took seriously the admonition that required three hours of preparation for each hour in class, a growing number of the present generation expect satisfactory grades, with or without understanding, with minimal preparation since higher education is just one part of their busy lives.

Many students have a low tolerance for frustration, and delayed gratification is a foreign concept. Some students view themselves as "consumers" who have "purchased" a product and expect it to be delivered to them in an acceptable fashion. They have high expectations regarding support services to make the process convenient and trouble-free.

As the focus of education shifts from the professor to the learner, developmental educators have a historic opportunity to reinvent themselves as resources for the entire campus-students and faculty alike—in partnering with the new enriched learning environment. The learning process must be expanded beyond the traditional classroom walls. The new process must be released from the shackles of the fixed number of traditional class time periods. Additional partners must be added to the learning environment in addition to the classroom professor.

Developmental educators are vital change agents in renewing the learning environment. Rather than being marginalised, the learning assistance profession is an essential partner within the campus learning community. Developmental education professionals have many of the skills needed for improved learning enrichment and higher graduation rates of students. Some of those skills include:

i) academic assessment,
ii) counselling,
iii) academic advisement,
iv) developing high school/college bridge programmes,
v) classroom assessment techniques,
vi) instructional technology,
vii) use of collaborative peer-assisted learning,
viii) adapting instruction to meet affective domain needs of diverse students,
ix) curriculum development,
x) program evaluation, and many others.

Numerous developmental education centres have been transformed into full service learning and teaching centres. In addition, some of these expanded centres also provide faculty development services as well. Learning assistance centres that have research-based evidence of positive student outcomes are viewed by many policy makers as important components of enrolment management and student retention programmes. Involving business and union leaders with the developmental education department advisory council may be powerful allies for supporting your efforts to secure institutional funding.

Students need to learn how to transfer specific strategies to the particular academic literacy demands of each course. Indeed, without effective training for transfer, college reading and learning courses face the very real danger of standing in isolation from the academic disciplines and of remaining mired in the deficit model. Many developmental educators possess knowledge and skills in one or more of the following areas:

i) peer collaborative learning,
ii) informal classroom assessment techniques,
iii) new paradigms of student learning pedagogy,
iv) instructional technology,
v) affective domain needs of students,
vi) curriculum development,
vii) peer reviews of teaching activities,
viii) professional development activities,
ix) adapting instruction for diverse learning styles, and other areas.

## Observational Assessment for Effective Teaching

Better teaching and learning requires the inclusion of assessment tools beyond the written test. Learning is a process as well as an end-state. To document learning, teachers must observe students as they learn: in a variety of settings, performing many activities, using a range of tools. Teaching involves more than the intellectual development of children. Teachers regularly work towards the emotional, physical, and aesthetic development of their students, as well as the development of social skills.

Observational assessment is equally valid and applicable in all of these learning domains. Observational assessment is a developing field with emerging methodologies. Conventional assessment puts a burden on students to prove what they learned in a setting isolated from the learning—usually, the written test. Since conventional assessment has been confined to a one-dimensional paper and pencil medium, it has little relevance to the actual cognitive challenges our students will encounter in life.

Conventional assessment is most often dependent upon the child's reading level. For students who have reading difficulties, conventional assessment fails to provide an accurate reflection of learning. Better teaching and learning requires the inclusion of assessment tools beyond the written test. Learning is a process as well as an end-state. To document learning, teachers must observe students as they learn: in a variety of settings, performing many activities, using a range of tools.

Observational assessment implies many changes in the way we teach and assess—a new paradigm for viewing the learning process. One intended change is that assessment becomes a formative, integral process of teaching in which ongoing assessments guide both teacher and learner. Teaching involves more than the intellectual development of children. Teachers regularly work towards the emotional, physical, and aesthetic development of their students, as well as the development of social skills.

Observational assessment is equally valid and applicable in all of these learning domains. Assessment relies on making observations that are both accurate and dependable. Though observations are subjective, there are many ways to achieve a high degree of accountability in designing your assessments. Observational assessment is accurate to the extent that it represents the learning outcome. One cannot infer the mastery of a complex capacity from the successful performance of a single task. To improve the accuracy of observations, teachers can:

i) Choose wording for observables that is clear to others.
ii) Design multiple and varied observables to assess mastery of a single learning outcome.
iii) Observe both simple and complex tasks in realistic settings.
iv) Choose tasks that are most generalisable to the learning outcome.
v) Match the observables to the outcomes as closely as possible.
vi) Share ideas with other colleagues involved with observational assessment.

Observers of any human behaviour should beware of the potential to "see what we want to see." This tendency may obscure seeing behaviours that are unexpected to the teacher, but significant for a learner. The more familiar the observer is with the subjects, the more this potential arises. An assessment is dependable to the extent that it can be observed accurately by other judges. Observables should be objective enough that multiple observers can make sufficiently similar judgments of the same performance. To improve the consistency of assessment of educational observables, teachers can:

i) Consider whether or not the wording of a comment requires too much inference or a conclusion that cannot be observed; observables should be just that—observable.
ii) Gather sufficient data to assess a learning outcome (use many observables in order to assess each outcome, reducing the influence of any single observable).
iii) Periodically use multiple judges to check the efficacy of your observables (and to share ideas with your colleagues).
iv) Share ideas with other colleagues involved in observational assessment.

For example, students may be given a paper-and-pencil test to determine their ability to name coins and find their sums, or be asked to run a classroom store using the coins, or be given real coins to play a game involving naming and sorting coins. By observing their ability to name coins and find their sums in a number of different settings, the teacher should have sufficient data to make a valid and reliable decision about the child's mastery of this skill.

Planning observables and making observations are inextricably linked together. Teachers both "plan to observe" and "observe in order to plan." This is an integrated, simultaneous process. When "planning to observe," teachers determine what skills or performances they wish to observe in their classroom. Some teachers use a few simple phrases, others make a detailed list of observables itemising the specific skills on which they are focusing.

Making observations is fundamental to both learning and teaching. Immediate documentation of learning provides more accurate information about learning and prevents later actions or events from influencing observations about learning. The observer should always be aware that anything observable is based upon the observer's interpretation of the world. It is important to be mindful of prejudices and continuously strive to maintain an open mind.

Learner Profile is an assessment tool that enables you to plan, organise, and review observations about students' progress and the work they produce. The package consists of powerful planning, analysis, and recording software. Learner Profile helps to make observational assessment practical for all educators.

Learner Profile includes a feature designed to improve the creation and planning of lessons using observables. Objectives, materials, activities, observable sets, assignments, and notes can be incorporated into lessons. The entire lesson plan or portions of the lesson may be printed. Learner Profile enables the observer to collect information that reflects student development and learning over time. As learning is observed, the observer describes the level of achievement by using a word or scale called a qualifier.

## References

Arendale, David, *Bridging the Gap of Teaching and Learning*, University of Missouri—Kansas City, 1997.

Chickering, A. W. and Gamson, Z. F., "Seven Principles of Good Practice in Undergraduate Education", *AAHE Bulletin*, 39, 3-7, 1987.

Hargreaves, D. H., "Teaching as a Research-based Profession: possibilities and prospects", *Teacher Training Agency Annual Lecture*, 1996.

Shneiderman, B., *Designing the user interface: Strategies for effective human-computer-interaction*, 1998.

# 4

# Classroom Cultures and Cultures in the Classroom

Students will be familiar with the appropriate interactional behaviours expected in the classroom. Some students are from cultures with values that promote field dependence, while other cultures are inclined to be field independent, which encourages independence and competition. With proper instruction, field-dependent and field-independent students can learn to be bicognitive; that is, their learning styles can be expanded to function appropriately in any given situation.

Teachers need to provide activities that incorporate all types of learning styles. If they are aware of their own cultural learning styles and preferences, teachers will be better prepared to recognise the learning styles of their students. Mainstream teachers are often at odds with their diverse students because they are unaware of the differing cultural values they bring to the classroom.

To promote effective teaching, teachers need to plan curriculum and instruction to incorporate the learning styles of their students. If students are uncomfortable in class, they may become bored, unresponsive, or test poorly. Based on cultural norms, participation structures describe the interactions of students in the classroom, when and how to speak, and what to speak about. Teachers may misinterpret inappropriate or awkward classroom interaction, as every culture has individual norms that dictate proper classroom behaviour and student-teacher interaction.

Miscommunication occurs during verbal interaction as well as through body language. Kinesics (the study of body language) includes facial expressions, posture, gestures, body movements, eye contact, or any ritual, that conveys messages or meaning for a culture. The Japanese bow is an example of kinesics. When the individuals bowing are equals in society, the bow is simultaneous and of the same depth. Every culture has its own way of depicting the following domains of non-linguistic communication:

i) *Paralinguistics*: Sounds that accompany language and vocalisations that replace speech.

ii) *Kinesics:* The study of body motion, gestures, unconscious body movement.

iii) *Oculesics:* Eye contact and motion to indicate meaning. Individuals from some cultures show respect and interest by making eye contact while other cultures show respect by not making eye contact.

iv) *Haptics:* Location, frequency, and contexts in which people touch.

v) *Proxemics:* The unconscious use and organisation of personal space.

vi) *Chronemics:* Perception and use of time.

vii) *Monochronic time:* Doing one thing at a time, in a linear fashion.

viii) *Polychronic time:* Doing many things at a time.

All cultures operate on their own systems of communication, and these beliefs will be manifested within the everyday context of the classroom. Knowledge of nonverbal communication specific to other cultures will help teachers to understand the students they teach, and well as students' parents. Educators must be careful not to make the mistake of judging people's emotions by using their own cultural indicators. Not everyone shows grief, anger, happiness, and embarrassment, or other emotions in the same manner. Students with teachers from their same culture have little problem understanding the cues provided by the teacher and the appropriate interactional behaviours expected in the classroom. Those children and teachers from differing cultures do not know the rules of each other's cultural rules and have difficulty interpreting correct teacher-student interactions.

Although not the panacea to end all classroom problems, effective teaching is more apt to take place if both the teacher and student are aware of the benefits of integrating appropriate instructional materials that correspond with culturally congruent teaching and learning styles. Knowing that cultural patterns drive behaviour, teachers who are aware that their students have differing cognitive styles are able to adapt their classrooms to include activities that incorporate all types of learning in their teaching. The teacher will begin to understand why some students experience problems when their natural learning styles are incompatible with the teaching style of the teacher.

Various researchers have pointed out that Asian students tend to be highly visual learners. Hispanics are generally auditory learners, and non-Westerners are more inclined to learn through tactile and kinesthetic modes. Individual personalities will always preside over the overarching cultural characteristics, yet teaching will be more effective and teachers can make modifications and adaptations to their curriculum and if they are aware of cultural differences.

For example, Islam is to be one of the fastest-growing religions in the United States and around the world, and is practised by Muslims. Many Americans consider themselves Muslims, and they are native speakers of English. Muslim students can be from any racial or ethnic background. Educators should be familiar with the fundamental beliefs of Muslims and make allowances for religious holidays, days of fasting, dietary requirements, prayer time and its accompanying rituals, expressions of personal modesty, and curriculum issues. The First Amendment of the US. Constitution protects the religious rights of individuals, which signifies that the classroom teacher should know as much as possible to foster understanding toward the Muslim student.

The fundamental religious aspects of Islam are reflected in the classroom, as are cultural aspects. The fundamental teachings of the *Quran,* characteristics of different ethnic groups that practice Islam might be similar, although the cultures might be very different. For example, Muslims from Malaysia are distinct from Muslims from Saudi Arabia, although they practise the same religion.

Respect for one another is of vital importance. Personal relationships, family, and friendship are central to life. For example, the American ways of forming relationships quickly, but superficially, are seen as having little depth or significance. Male/female relationships are restricted and are governed by a rigid set of cultural rules.

Teachers need to be knowledgeable about how to respect the rights and beliefs of these students. Modesty is prescribed for post-pubescent boys and girls when dealing with the opposite sex. Shaking hands with the opposite sex, even if it is a teacher or administrator, for example, might be viewed as immodest, as well as co-ed physical education classes and school dances. No pressure to participate should be exhibited, nor should students be penalised for refusing to take part in these mixed gender activities.

Muslim children are prohibited from uncovering their bodies and are not allowed to participate in communal showers after sports. Private showers should be available, and if the class is scheduled late in the day, students should be allowed to skip the showers altogether and wait until they get home. Physical education clothing should be modified so that the girls wear full tracksuits, and the boys wear knee-length shorts. Mixed sex swimming classes are a problem for Muslim students. They should not be penalised for non-participation on religious grounds.

Teachers and administrators need to protect the student's personal and religious right to wear a scarf, and should prohibit and reprimand classmates who pull or remove a Muslim girl's scarf. Since Islam has its own specific set of teachings about human development and related issues, parents need the option to remove their children from any family life programmes offered by the schools.

Students who are fasting can be excused from going to the cafeteria at lunchtime and from participating in strenuous physical activity. In an effort to support multiculturalism in the community, the teacher can seize this teachable moment by inviting guest speakers to teach the other students about the rituals observed in a variety of religions. Muslim parents may teach their children to stand up, but perhaps not salute the flag when reciting the pledge because Islam discourages acts that are irreverent to God. This is not meant to be offensive or a symbol of disrespect to the symbol of the nation.

In Asian countries, parents teach their children to respect authority, feel responsibility for relatives, and show self-control. School failure is seen as a lack of will, and this failure can be alleviated by increasing parental restrictions. These children appear to be more dependent, conforming, and obedient by placing the family's welfare before their own desires.

Asian cultures also value the idea of humility and/or self-effacement. Children may not volunteer to participate in the classroom until specifically asked by the teacher. Drawing attention to oneself by virtue of misbehaving might cause great distress and result in "losing face" because children are taught to value silence, listen more than speak, speak softly, and be modest in dress and behaviour.

Learning styles of Black children tend to be more field dependent. Field dependent learners are more people and teacher oriented, more spontaneous, flexible, and less structured in perceptions of people, thoughts, and events. Field independent learners are more accustomed to working alone, may be are more competitive, are objective and task oriented, and think analytically and in a linear pattern.

Patterns are transmitted through black community tradition, pressure to conform to mainstream society, and structure conditions as a result of being placed at the bottom rung of society's ladder. Historically, skills and language were transmitted orally from one generation to the next, resulting in a distinctive culture. Consequently, this myriad of social issues has contributed profoundly to the personality development, attitudes, behaviours, and psychological characteristics of Blacks.

## Changing Classroom Cultures

Curriculum can now be developed around needs and interests of students, which facilitates critical thinking. Online projects allow classrooms to become more student based and less teacher directed. The ownership and literal connectivity students feel with online projects and communication make learning more effective. The WWW and educational applications allow for global collaboration, school wide curriculum integration, and student teacher connectivity.

The internet has become an integral part of our school curriculum, communication and teaching methods. It has become an intertwining tool that threads our school community together. Local leaders, parents and community role models were contacted to collect information. This added a new perspective and forged a strong working relationship between students and the local community. Collaborative projects using the internet also discourage the competition between technologically advanced students and students who do not have computers at home. Students are aware of who computer "experts" are and enter the classroom with a lower level of computer confidence. This is where the role of the teacher is crucial.

Globally, online projects allow students to look into the lives of students their own age and of varying life situations. This broadens their world of understanding and opens up physical and symbolic lines of communication. With Online projects such as cyberfair, inquiry based research, virtual field trips, and peer editing writing groups students are able to reach out to other cultures, perspectives and ideas. Newspapers and online resources became an important part of students lives because they wanted to see what was happening in the lives of their peers around the world.

With online collaborative projects, students work in an environment, which is free of judgment, racism, religious preference and socio-economic standards. Yet, inevitably students bring their life views to the project and are able to expose students to different perspectives. There are very specific online collaborative projects that are designed for teachers to work with. All of which allow students to be exposed to and correspond with students from all over the world.

An inquiry based collaborative internet research project that allows students to explore their own interests as a small group. As a class, discussions about the validity of web sites, the author's legitimacy, and the overall standard of information within websites was necessary. A guide for determining the validity and usefulness of a webpage was developed and adhered to. A working navigational log and bibliography of useful and not so useful sites helped students track their research and become more efficient with their research. This was the first step in allowing students to use the internet to think critically. It was up to the students to decide how to uncover and effectively utilise the information they were collecting.

Teens were naturally drawn to topics of drug abuse, AIDS, political movements and the environment, all of which present extremely opposing ideas. Students thought critically to sort through the abundance of information and to confirm their thoughts and ideas with experts in their field. This is a skill that textbooks cannot teach students. They learned to become critically literate readers and thinkers by actually doing the work instead of reading about doing the work. The work connects directly with a student's interests and is not simply chosen by a textbook editor. This therefore makes the activity more effective.

For educators, the internet allows teaching to shift from textbooks to real life experiences. Learning about different cultures and situations no longer are one-dimensional, but rounded and textual. School curriculum can now incorporate methods of reaching children of different learning styles as well as allowing students to convey their ideas in a context that suits their needs. Whether it is a spreadsheet, a web page or a multimedia presentation, it is creating meaning for and by individual students. With the use of proper assessment such as electronic portfolios, learning logs, and teacher student interviews, both teacher and students are able to let learning happen in new and innovative ways.

It is very easy for students to take information off the internet and call it their own. It is mandatory that teachers take the time to interview students, to review their portfolios and to ask the questions of why and how. How do the students know that the information that they learned online is valid? Why do they think other students see the world in such a different way? It is an opportunity to truly create critical thinkers and learners.

Students are learning when technology is a tool and when it is a distraction. As a teacher, it is readily accessible to see how learning is taking place. It eliminates the focus of learning how to use computers and shifts the concentration to how to utilise computers as a tool to express a higher level of learning. There is no better way to provide professional development for teachers as they begin to see the potential of collaborative projects. It allows teacher to step out of the forefront and guide students in using technology critically to become life long learners.

Many teachers who are not familiar with technology have a fear of using the internet as a teaching tool. Teachers can work closely with students and other educators to reach educational goals and standards. Teachers will then be inclined and encouraged to incorporate online projects into the curriculum. With the numerous sites that match teachers up and mentor them through the process, there is little room for apprehension.

A technology aware teacher can be paired with another teacher to complete a collaborative project together. Teachers can work as mentors to each other exposing new teachers to the wonders of learning with the internet. Eventually teachers develop the confidence to create their own online projects to further the individual needs of each student. This is especially helpful in customising the education for students with special needs.

## References

Bareth, L. G. & Manning, M.L., *Multicultural Education of Children and Adolescents*, Needham Heights, MA: Allyn and Bacon, 1992.

Carrasquillo, A., *Hispanic children and youth in the United States: A Resource Guide*, New York: Garland, 1991.

Cena, Johanna E., Bridging Gaps Between Cultures, Classrooms and Schools: A Close Look at Online Collaborative Learning, *Educational Technology & Society* 3(3) 2000.

Cox, B.G, and Ramirez, M., "Cognitive styles: Implications for multiethnic education", In J. Banks, (Ed.), *Education in the 80's: Implications for multiethnic education*, Washington, DC: National Education Association, 1981.

Gollnick, D.M, & and Chin, P.C., *Multicultural education in a pluralistic society (5 th edition)*, New Jersey: Prentice Hall, 1998.

Ramirez, M., & Castañeda, A., *Cultural democracy, bicognitive development and education*, p. 169-170. New York: Academic Press, 1974.

Tharp, R., "Culturally compatible education: A formula for designing effective classrooms", In H. Trueba, G. Spindler, & L. Spindler (Eds.), *What do anthropologists have to say about dropouts*? New York: Falmer Press, 1989.

Tharp, R., "Psychocultural variables and constants: Effects on teaching and learning in schools", *American Psychologist*, 44, (2), 349-359, February, 1989.

# 5

# Evaluation of Teaching

The evaluation of teaching can have important consequences for both students and teachers. This is not a science; there is still much to learn. These evaluations have substantial influence in administrative decisions such as faculty tenure, promotion, and post-tenure reviews. On the other hand, teaching evaluations provide feedback to instructors about their pedagogical strengths and weaknesses. Student questionnaires are, by far, the most popular form of teaching feedback. These paper-and-pencil tools are easy to tabulate and economical to administer, but they are also the most controversial evaluation tool, due to common problems in their design and implementation.

A mid-term evaluation can consist of only a conventional student questionnaire, but this feedback technique is very commonly augmented with interviews, debriefing sessions and follow-up questionnaires. From a pedagogical perspective, there is evidence that mid-term evaluations are substantial improvements over end-of-term questionnaires. Some study shows that students are more satisfied with mid-term evaluations.

The most common form of mid-term evaluation is the Small Group Instructional Diagnosis (SGID). Despite all the benefits that student feedback can bring to the classroom, the use of student evaluations for instructional improvement is dismally infrequent. Reasons for the infrequent use of student evaluations to improve teaching can probably be traced to the concerns that many instructors harbour about the fairness and usefulness of these surveys. The mandatory use of student evaluations lead "to a significant reduction in faculty morale and job satisfaction."

Formative applications are those where student evaluations are used as a tool for instructional improvement. There is substantial agreement among researchers that student evaluations provide consistent feedback of general areas of an instructor's strengths and weaknesses, and can result in substantial improvement of specific target areas. One of the most researched issues in teaching evaluations is whether an instructor can increase his/her ratings by giving undeserved high grades to students.

There is no simple system for evaluating the quality of faculty research, there is no simple system for evaluating the quality of faculty teaching. However, by thinking carefully about the purposes of evaluation, and by crafting multiple methods of evaluation that suit those purposes, one can devise evaluation systems that are reliable, valid, and fair. Equally important, the process of discussing and crafting evaluation systems focuses attention on the practice of good teaching and helps to create a culture in which teaching is highly valued.

## PRINCIPLES OF TEACHING EVALUATION

*Multiple methods*: The most important consideration in teaching evaluation, both for improvement purposes and for personnel decisions, is the use of multiple methods of teaching evaluation involving multiple sources of data.

*Faculty, departmental and school responsibilities*: To ensure that the evaluation system adopted is credible and acceptable, faculty members must have a strong hand in its development. Before departments and schools adopt teaching evaluation systems, the faculty members should determine their criteria for effective teaching. Departments and schools can then take responsibility for developing their own evaluation methods and evaluation criteria.

Since different disciplines require different methods and settings for instruction, they require different methods and criteria for evaluation. This is also true for interdisciplinary instruction. Teaching evaluation systems can be flexible to accommodate diversity in instructional methods (e.g., lecture, discussion, lab, case study, small group interaction, practicum, studio, field work, clinical work, etc.). To promote compatibility within the university, standards should be reviewed, understood, and accepted by all groups involved in the promotion and tenure review process.

*Individualising teaching evaluation*: Effective teaching evaluation must be individualised. A uniform system discriminates against some individuals, so a plan sensitive to individual variation should be developed. A faculty member should provide information about his/her contributions and accomplishments as a teacher on a longitudinal basis over his/her teaching career. Consideration can then be given to changes in emphasis and interest that will naturally occur in an academic career.

*What may be assessed*: Teaching evaluation has as its central element the assessment of the quality of classroom instruction. Since teaching includes activities broader than classroom instruction, evaluation of teaching must assess more than classroom performance. While schools may identify additional items, among the teaching activities that may be assessed are the following:

i) quality, amount, and level of classroom instruction (including shared instruction);
ii) development of curricula, new courses, and classroom materials;
iii) supervision and mentoring of graduate students, including chairing of dissertations;
iv) service on graduate examination and dissertation committees;
v) one-on-one consultation with students, including supervision of independent study and readings courses;
vi) supervision of teaching assistants in undergraduate courses;
vii) conduct and supervision of laboratory instruction;

viii) supervision of undergraduate and graduate research;
ix) advising students in the major;
x) supervision of field work; and
xi) supervision of clinical and practicum experiences.

Throughout the term, faculty members may act as "classroom researchers," gathering measures of student learning in order to improve their teaching. Faculty may also wish to provide examples of student learning as evidence of their teaching effectiveness for personnel decisions. In most institutions, faculty and administrators have relied on student ratings of teaching effectiveness for teaching improvement purposes and for personnel decisions.

Colleagues can provide important evaluative information through classroom visits. In particular, a colleague's observation of such aspects of teaching as appropriateness of materials and methods, breadth and depth of material covered, the relation of such material to the syllabus and goals of the course, and incorporation of recent developments in the discipline can offer a more informed appraisal of the instructor's mastery of content than can students' perceptions.

There is consensus that peer observation has enjoyed more success as a strategy for teaching improvement than for personnel decisions. When used for personnel decisions, it is important to have explicit criteria by which colleagues make evaluations. Colleagues can evaluate course materials, such as syllabi, textbooks, handouts, assignments, graded exams, graded papers, etc. In the visual and performing arts, colleagues may evaluate faculty-directed art exhibits, theater and dance productions, musical ensembles, and individual performances when these activities are directly related to a faculty member's instructional activities.

Colleagues may be in the most advantageous position to evaluate such teaching-related activities as curriculum development, supervision of student research, participation in colleagues' and teaching assistants' teaching development, articles on teaching in disciplinary journals and other publications, and authorship of textbooks and other instructional materials.

The development of a teaching dossier (or portfolio) is a method that allows individuals to collect and display multiple sources of information regarding their teaching effectiveness for examination by others. It contributes both to sound personnel decisions and to the professional development of individual faculty members. A dossier is a factual description of a professor's major strengths and teaching achievements. The purpose of the dossier will drive decisions about format and content. The purpose will also guide decisions about what materials will be reviewed and by whom. There is no single prescription for how a teaching dossier should be structured or what specific information it should contain. Each unit will need to decide what is important and relevant.

**Evidence-based Teaching**

Educational research and ongoing evaluation must be considered as a fundamental part of educational advance. The trends in the evidence based medicine, educational bodies are concerned with building a body of best evidence in medical education (BEME). A meeting in London was held in 1999 highlighting the need for evidence-based teaching. Although this initiative is in the medical field, successful strategies could well be extended into the dental field. There are six steps in the practice of evidence-based teaching:

i) framing the question,
ii) developing a search strategy,
iii) producing the raw data,
iv) evaluating the evidence,
v) implementing change and
vi) evaluating

The difficulty of evaluating any educational philosophy in a scientific manner is highlighted by the many different methodologies used in attempts to prove the efficacy of problem based learning (PBL) as a life-long learning resource. One of the most frustrating aspects of evaluating education is that academics in the medical and dental field, who have been trained in the rigid scientific methods which are mandatory for evaluating treatment modalities, are tempted to try to transpose such methods to evaluating education. Such attempts, while superficially pleasing in the numerical data they supply, are ultimately unreliable.

The rigid quantitative scientific method of controlled experimentation cannot be considered valid in an environment where the variables of the subject pool are almost as great or greater than the pool itself, the student pool in any one year of a dental or medical school being statistically minute. While the subject pool is small, prior knowledge, motivation, opportunity, access to materials, the Hawthorne effect, time constraints, emotional status and even financial pressure can count among the influences affecting learning. Including sequential years and/or different schools can confuse the issue further by adding the variable of different student cultures.

Currently, the most pragmatic approach in educational evaluation is to focus on students' perception of their experience with a learning program, and this approach has been used in several studies. Enjoyment and success engender a winning cycle in the learning environment. If teaching resources can involve students and lead them to be successful in their endeavours, they are more likely enjoy their tasks and want to become even more involved. Exploring students perceptions lends itself to a qualitative research methodology, the focus of which is understanding rather than measuring.

Qualitative research can tap into the students' psyche to give a depth of understanding that is the key for ongoing educational development. It is particularly germane to evaluation of the formative aspect of a program and should be part of the development of any educational resource. Good qualitative research goes beyond reporting what people say to why they are saying it. It makes a distinction between public and spoken attitudes which are socially acceptable, or those which may have no vocabulary or are difficult to verbalise and are therefore suppressed, and private attitudes which may not be socially acceptable and are therefore consciously repressed.

Qualitative researchers in the commercial field require a high level of expertise to avoid a host of pitfalls and qualitative research methodology has its own strict guidelines. In an educational context it would be imperative that questionnaires dealing with students' perceptions are anonymous and that focus groups be conducted by people known to be far removed from any summative assessment results. Observation of students involved in a programme is another invaluable developmental device. However, this is a subjective activity and, with a single observer, is only as valid as the perception of that observer.

Quantitative analysis of factors which have been found to be relevant to students via this exploratory research can then proceed, each small positive outcome accumulating to build a broad picture of what is likely to produce success. Triangulation, which is the application and combination of several research methodologies in the study of the same phenomena can be employed in both quantitative (validation) and qualitative (inquiry) studies. It has been proposed that, by combining multiple observers, theories, methods and empirical materials, researchers can hope to overcome the weakness or intrinsic biases of any particular methodology and the problems that come from single method, single-observer, single-theory studies.

Students might routinely evaluate the teaching they experience in college was a hard sell on most campuses; student ratings were usually introduced with a good deal of struggle. The controversies over the years caused student ratings to become the most extensively studied aspect of collegiate education. Even today, though, student evaluations seldom make an optimal contribution to improving either teaching or personnel decisions.

Student ratings of teaching should encourage students to think about their educational experiences—to develop clearer conceptions of the kinds of teaching and educational experiences that contribute most to their learning.

An alternative to a rating form is Small Group Instructional Diagnosis, in which a consultant observes, a class session and then conducts discussions with students about what is helping or hindering their learning. The observer summarises the information and provides consultative help to the instructor. This is particular helpful because students find out that other students not only perceive the situation differently from themselves but also may have different needs. The SGID is usually carried out between the first third and middle of a term. One benefit of collecting midterm impressions of a course from students is that the students can actually experience the effect of any suggestions the instructor implements; thus they are likely to be motivated to give helpful feedback

Student involvement will have progressively less impact if aspects of a course or curriculum have not been changed despite generations of student complaints. There are undoubtedly times when the faculty knows better than students what is needed, but a long record of student complaints signals at the least that we've done a poor job of helping them understand why the course or curriculum is as it is. In short, the student opinion form could, and should, be educational in the highest sense—helping students gain a better understanding of the goals of education, stimulating them to think more metacognitively about their own learning, motivating them to continue learning, and encouraging them to accept responsibility for their learning.

Teaching is a highly personal activity, involving one's deepest sense of self. Research on feedback from filmed or videotaped classes has shown that the teacher viewing the videotape tends to focus on minutiae of gestures and personal appearance. The videotape can help a teacher sort out the major issues from the minutiae. Similarly, in interpreting student ratings, a consultant can help sort out the most useful information, provide encouragement and strategies for improvement, and suggest printed materials, workshops, training opportunities, or other means for continued learning.

Student ratings also are used in decisions about promotion and salary increases. Clearly, teaching methods, and therefore ratings, differ across departments. Similarly, even though variables such as class size, grading standards, class level, and other characteristics have relatively small effects upon overall student ratings, small differences in numerical averages are often treated as significant by personnel committees, because norms are so often detrimental to teacher motivation and are so frequently misused in personnel decisions.

Student ratings may be the best-validated source of evidence of teaching effectiveness. Today the most frequently advocated device is the teaching dossier or portfolio. The portfolio approach has many advantages, including that of providing diverse sources of evidence. Portfolios can, however, be costly to put together, in time and resources, and they have their own sources of bias. An "attractive" portfolio—with colour, graphics, and perhaps a videotape—may prove more persuasive than one with less polish. The nature of effective teaching differs across disciplines, the nature of portolios should vary, too.

## Impact of Teacher Preparation System

The impact on the system of teacher preparation was immediate and profound. Many preparation programs were flooded with candidates who were already classroom teachers and who were looking for assistance on how to teach tomorrow. Incentives for students to complete their programs before entering the profession simply disappeared on many campuses as job offers came flooding in from local district administrators desperate to find an adult to head each classroom. On the policy front, institutions of higher education came under pressure to increase the number of new credential recipients and to increase the quality of their preparation programs.

Within the current changing political and economic contexts, teacher preparation programs are facing a series of conflicting challenges. The specific provisions and implementation timeline are different for different teachers, depending on whether they are new to the profession or not; whether they teach elementary, middie, or high school.

The new credentialing system consists of two parts: teacher preparation and induction. Teacher preparation involves the courses and assessments teachers take to earn a preliminary credential, and induction occurs during the first 2 years of teaching, when teachers take courses and the assessments necessary to earn a professional credential. The trend in the production of special education teachers has not matched the growth of single- and multiple-subject credentials.

The growth in special education credentials has been largely in intern credentials. In fact, the production of fully credentialed special education teachers has actually decreased over the past few years as demand has risen. The fact that almost one in five special education teachers do not hold at least a preliminary special education credential is critical because of the specialised knowledge and skills needed to work with this population of students.

Interns are working teachers who participate in structured programs to complete the coursework and other requirements for a full credential. Pre-interns are working teachers who participate in programs designed to help them meet the requirements for entering an intern program. They are not yet enrolled in a teacher preparation program.

There are many routes into the teaching profession in all over the world. The so-called traditional route has historically been the most common path: after earning an undergraduate degree, prospective teachers complete a year of coursework, student teach, and then earn a credential. Some progress through their program full-time, while others go part-time, often taking convenient night-time classes. "Alternative-route" is a term coined to describe a variety of routes into the profession that share the common experience that participants begin to teach before they earn a credential.

The intern route is for individuals who have demonstrated subject matter competency. The program typically involves prescribed coursework, as in the traditional program, along with some support through a mentor and sometimes collaborative meetings. Pre-intern programs serve not fully credentialed teachers who have not yet demonstrated subject matter competency. Typically, these programs aim to help teachers prepare to pass subject matter competency tests.

Some programs also require that pre-interns attend a certain series of workshops covering topics outside of test preparation, such as classroom management. Other programs have a mentoring component designed to provide pre-interns with support at their school site. The emergency "route" is not a route at all-it is an *ad hoc* and individual arrangement in which classroom teachers without credentials need do no more than show they have pursued minimal coursework requirements each year. Emergency-permit teachers tend to proceed part-time through traditional programs, which, of course, have not been designed with their needs in mind. Regardless of whether teachers take a traditional, an alternative, or an emergency route into teaching, they need to meet the same basic requirements for a preliminary credential.

There can be great variation within each route because prospective teachers' experiences can vary dramatically. Their courses may be demanding or not, field experiences may be valuable or not, and the teacher candidates may or may not take full advantage of their opportunities to learn. Teacher candidates may complete the program in a year, or they may be enrolled in the program part-time, just take a course or two at a time, and stretch their preparation out over many years.

Coursework requirements are basically equal for traditional and alternative-route credential candidates; in fact, these different types of students are often taking the same classes side by side. The key difference is whether courses are taken before or during their first few years of teaching, often making for dramatically different teacher preparation experiences. Interns and others' who are teaching while taking teacher preparation courses can face extremely burdensome schedules.

Student teaching is considered by many to be a particularly important part of teacher preparation. It is also the area of teacher preparation where alternative and traditional routes appear to diverge most significantly. In a traditional program, student teaching ideally involves many hours of observing in an experienced teacher's classroom and gradually assuming more responsibility for instruction. The student teacher's first attempts at teaching are typically all under the guidance of the more experienced teacher, who can then provide feedback on the strengths and weaknesses of the student teacher's performance. In alternative programs, the "student teacher" is already teaching and thus does not have as much time to observe veterans.

Student teaching is the culminating experience in the program-so those who entered teaching as an intern would not typically student teach until their fourth semester as a classroom teacher. For the three semesters prior to student teaching, the nontraditional student may receive some support from a mentor, but not the amount of time observing and being coached that is possible in the traditional model. A few intern programs require interns to student teach during their summer break or when they are off-track, so that, in a sense, they complete "traditional" student teaching as the final requirement in their credential program.

However, in the majority of programs, teachers "student teach" in their own classrooms with a university or district supervising teacher completing a required number of observations. Given the differences in what it means to "student teach" in traditional and nontraditional programs, it is not surprising that traditional- and nontraditional-route teachers report different student teaching experiences. Traditional teacher preparation programs provide far more opportunity for collaborating with the supervising teacher on lesson plans and far more opportunities to observe an experienced teacher in the classroom. Of course, not all traditionally prepared teachers benefit from their student teaching, and not all nontraditionally prepared teachers are less effective because their student teaching experience was different.

Traditionally prepared teachers complete their coursework, earn their credentials, and then begin to teach. Interns also typically receive some type of formal on-the-job support from their programs. This is one of the major strengths of such programs and, when well implemented, can provide teachers the practical assistance they need to succeed while they are completing their preparation. In contrast, teachers on emergency permits often do not receive formal mentoring or on-the-job support. Pre-interns may or may not receive mentoring or other support for teaching, and the mentoring they receive, if any, appears to be of mixed quality. Pre-interns, like teachers on emergency-permits, often have to rely on their own initiative to access informal supports.

Teaching full-time and earning a credential at the same time is difficult, whether the teacher holds an emergency permit or is enrolled in a pre-intern or intern program. The majority of alternative-route teachers said they entered teaching without completing preparation programs because a teaching opportunity came up, they could not afford a full-time program, they already had some form of teaching experience, or they did not want to give up income while attending a preparation program. Very few teachers decided to begin teaching without completing a credential because they felt that preparation was "basically a formality" that would not improve their job performance.

## References

Corcoran, T. B., *Helping teachers teach well: transforming professional development*, New Brunswick, NJ: Center for Policy Research in Education, Rutgers University, 1995.

Lechner, Sybille K., *Evaluation of Teaching and Learning Strategies,* 2001.

Lechner S.K., Lechner K.M, Thomas G.A., "Evalua-tion of a computer aided learning program in prosthodontics", *J Prosthodont* 1999:7 (2):100-105.

Little, J. W., "Teachers' professional development in a climate of educational reform", *Educational Evaluation and Policy Analysis,* 15(2), 129-151, 1993.

Long A.F., Mercer P.E., Stephens C.D. et al, "The evaluation of three computer-assisted learning packages for general dental practitioners", *Brit Dent J* 1994;177:410-5

Mulligan R., Wood G.J., "A controlled evalua-tion of computer assisted training simulations in geriatric dentistry", *J Dent Educ* 1993.

Rice, J., *Teacher quality: understanding the effectiveness of teacher attributes,* Washington, DC: Economic Policy Institute, 2003.

Riehl, L., Young, V., *Final report of the independent evaluation of the Beginning Teacher Support and Assessment Program (BTSA),* San Francisco, CA: WestEd, 2002.

Sefton A., "Evaluating the new technologies", *Proceedings of Evaluating New Teaching Technologies,* Uniserve Science, Sydney.

Wilkes M, Bligh J., "Evaluating educational in-terventions", *Brit Med J* 1999; 318:1269-1272.

# 6

# Contemporary Research on Teaching

History of education reform has shown that innovations have failed dramatically when teachers input was not incorporated and when teachers were not actively involved in the innovation. Therefore, for successful integration of computers in primary schools, it is essential that the organised body of teachers participates in the decision making process, as well as in the design, implementation, and evaluation of programs relating to this innovation.

## Technology Integration in Schools

Technology has the potential to support curriculum and policy reform. However, reform efforts alone will not cause the necessary change. There is a reciprocal relation between reform and technology. For successful technology integration in schools, teacher education programs play a crucial role. Teacher preparation on technologies should provide teachers with a solid understanding of the various media, their affordances, and their constraints. Such understandings can only emerge when teachers are actively involved in teaching and learning with technology across the various disciplines.

Technology skills should not be taught out of context. One can best learn how to use a computer while working on a meaningful task. Teacher preparation should not be based on training for "computer literacy" but should prepare teachers for using technologies to construct, represent, and share knowledge in real life authentic contexts. Teachers should not be taught about technology but how to use technology for constructing, organising, and communicating knowledge.

A long history of technology use in education shows that the first inclination is to use new technology in the same traditional ways as the old technology. Continuing old practices with new technology will neither change nor improve education. Old curricula and pedagogical approaches should be reformed, and if necessary replaced, to take advantage of the affordances of the new media. According to constructivism, knowledge doesn't exist external to the learner. Rather, individual learners construct their own meanings based on their prior experiences. Learning is a result of construction, collaboration, reflection, and negotiation within a rich context in which learning is situated.

Technology has the potential to support constructivist learning and be used for active, authentic, and cooperative activities. Knowledge building results when learners interact with their peers, collaborate, discuss their ideas, form arguments, and negotiate meaning. When used appropriately, technology provides a more decentralised environment where students take more control of the learning environment and become active constructors of knowledge while working on authentic tasks.

Information technologies and computer networks shift the role of the teacher from knowledge transmitter to that of a facilitator who provides opportunities for interaction and meaning making to all learners. Technologies are not deliverers of content, but tools that educators and students use to construct knowledge and share meaning. The use of technology and cultural tools to communicate, exchange information, and construct knowledge is fundamental in constructivism. Strategies for teaching and learning are not chosen to facilitate transfer of knowledge from the world to the learner's head, but to provide tools the learner will use to create meaning.

Teachers should therefore be trained to use computers in ways that will allow their students to construct knowledge.

Technology-based learning occurs when students use computers as mindtools that enable them to represent what they know and organise their knowledge in meaningful ways. Mind tools are tools that aid and extend the user's thinking capabilities and can be used for knowledge construction and problem solving. Some examples of mind tools include computer conferencing, databases, spreadsheets, and hypermedia development tools.

Such conceptions of technology-based teaching and learning should drive the reform efforts of teacher preparation and in-service teacher professional development. If we adopt a constructivist approach to teacher education, evaluation practices need to be reformed as well. Constructivist environments promote the creation of multiple perspectives within a variety of contexts. There is not one correct understanding and there is not one correct way of solving a problem.

Students are encouraged to utilise multiple ways of solving instructional problems and justify their solutions. The creation of multiple perspectives and viewpoints calls for multiple assessment methods. In a teacher education course, a variety of evaluation techniques can provide information about the learners' thinking processes, self-reflective skills, performance in completing real-world authentic tasks, and the ability to identify technology solutions to instructional problems.

Traditional tests can also be used but they should not be the only method of evaluation. Other evaluation techniques include the collection of students' projects and assignments, students' self-evaluations, reflective journals, and class presentations of sample lessons. When the teacher educator employs such evaluation techniques, she also models for prospective teachers appropriate evaluation strategies of constructivist learning.

Technology should be an integral part of teacher preparation programmes. Research shows that teachers tend to teach the way that they were taught. In a course on educational technology for teachers, the goal should not simply be to teach the use of several technology systems, their advantages, and disadvantages. Instead, the goal should be to provide students with opportunities to think like experts in making instructional decisions, selecting media for appropriate use, structuring learning activities, and employing sound pedagogical strategies in real-life contexts.

The instructor in a teacher preparation course should structure the learning environment so that she will have the opportunity to model expert behaviour to students in sound uses of technology-based teaching and learning. It is important that the teacher educator is an expert in technology-based learning because only then she can model to her students—future teachers—expert behaviour.

There are numerous ways of integrating technology in teacher education since technology can provide a rich context for learning. Technology rich environments allow prospective teachers to experience real-life scenarios of classroom teaching, construct multiple perspectives, and reflect on their practice. Several rich interactive multimedia systems exist in the market that allow students to work in groups to review video vignettes of classroom teaching, identify good practices, and discuss them with their peers.

Curriculum, pedagogical, and policy changes are essential for the success of reform. To effectively integrate technology in teaching, pre-service teachers need to be well prepared, but also in-service teachers need to deepen their knowledge and skills as well. In-service teachers need time to develop, master, and reflect on technology-based learning approaches. They need time and incentives to participate in lifelong professional development.

Changing the teacher compensation structures and providing incentives can encourage teachers to participate in professional development activities throughout their careers and develop lifelong learning skills. Another policy reform that can help promote professional development is to incorporate the completion of training attended to career ladder programs. In addition, a skills-based or competency-based compensation pay system might be a better way to value and reward teacher knowledge and skills. In such a system, teachers with more experience in the classroom and teachers who completed more professional development hours would get higher salaries. Such an approach can send the message to teachers that new skills are needed and valued, that the ministry is willing to compensate them for committing the time to improve their skills, and that for schools to continue educating our children, teachers need to develop lifelong learning habits which will enhance their professional knowledge.

**Effectiveness of Technology Integration**

There are a number of reasons to track the effectiveness of technology integration. The integration of technology into a school is in many ways like its integration into any business setting. Technology is a tool to improve productivity and practice. Measures need to be available to assess effectiveness, and yet some of the most significant effects can be difficult to measure. For administrative tasks, technology can improve worker productivity by removing repetitive aspects of complex tasks or improving system communication.

Technology integration in the classroom also has the potential to support important educational goals. Technology, it has been argued, helps change teacher-student relationships, encourages project-based learning styles, and supports the acquisition of skills such as "higher order thinking," analysis, and problem solving. The most important reason for measuring, though, is the understanding that the impact of technology on schools is dependent upon how successfully technology is integrated.

Technology integration is the incorporation of technology resources and technology-based practices into the daily routines, work, and management of schools. Technology resources are computers and specialised software, network-based communication systems, and other equipment and infrastructure. Practices include collaborative work and communication, internet-based research, remote access to instrumentation, network-based transmission and retrieval of data, and other methods.

Integrating technology is what comes next after making the technology available and accessible. It is a goal-in-process, not an end state. The goal of perfect technology integration is inherently unreachable: technologies change and develop, students and teachers come and go,and things change. It is the process by which people and their institutional setting adapt to the technology that matters most.

The process of technology integration is one of continuous change, learning, and (hopefully) improvement. Developing a culture that embraces technology is also important to its successful integration; for example, sending important messages by e-mail, or encouraging staff to use electronic calendars to schedule meetings, fosters a culture that accepts technology as "natural" to the business of everyday work.

The issue of the desirability of technology integration relates to the links between technology adoption and educational or management outcomes. The lists of observable behaviours can be used by school and district personnel to think about what to measure, and consideration of what to measure in turn leads to thinking about how to measure it.

The goal of placing technology in the classroom is to provide new ways for students to learn. Proper integration of technology will make the technology support these new ways of learning transparently. When students are able to choose and use technology tools to help themselves obtain information, analyse, synthesise, and assimilate it, and then present it in an acceptable manner, then technology integration has taken place.

Establishing and implementing technology literacy standards for students can help guide teacher efforts to integrate technology. The following are the construction skill competencies for elementary school students:

i) Use computer-based writing tools to communicate thoughts, ideas, and stories.

ii) Use computer-based drawing tools to illustrate thoughts, ideas, and stories.

iii) Use digital cameras to illustrate thoughts, ideas, and stories.

iv) Use multimedia authoring tools in the creation of knowledge products.

v) Use presentation software in the creation of knowledge products.

vi) Use WWW authoring tools in the creation of knowledge products.

vii) Use audio tapes for self-directed and/or extended learning.

viii) Use videos for self-directed and/or extended learning.

ix) Use technology resources for self-directed and/or extended learning.

x) Use technology resources for problem solving.

xi) Create non-print media for personal fulfilment.

xi) Explain basic strategies for revising, improving and updating non-print media.

xii) Use telecommunications technologies to participate in collaborative projects.

xiii) Work collaboratively to seek and/or communicate information in non-print formats.

xiv) Work collaboratively to create simple nonprint information products.

Administrators will benefit from understanding and competently using technology themselves as they lead a school or district and set priorities. Experience as a hands-on user helps administrators understand the change process that schools must undergo and the requirements for successful technology integration. Effectively applying technology empowers administrators to manage with information and make data-driven educational decisions.

Standards for administrators identify a common focus for the role of leadership in enhancing learning and school operations through the use of technology.

Educational leaders inspire a shared vision for comprehensive integration of technology and foster an environment and culture conducive to the realisation of that vision. Educational leaders ensure that curricular design, instructional strategies, and learning environments integrate appropriate technologies to maximise learning and teaching.

Educational leaders apply technology to enhance their professional practice and to increase their own productivity and that of others. Educational leaders ensure the integration of technology to support productive systems for learning and administration. They use technology to plan and implement comprehensive systems of effective assessment and evaluation.

Educational leaders understand the social, legal, and ethical issues related to technology and model responsible decision-making related to these issues. Superintendents who effectively lead integration of technology typically perform the following tasks:

i) establish a culture that encourages responsible risk-taking with technology while requiring accountability for results.
ii) maintain an emphasis on technology fluency among staff across the district and provide staff development opportunities to support high expectations.
iii) use current information tools and systems for communication, management of schedules and resources, performance assessment, and professional learning.

District program directors who effectively lead integration of technology typically perform the following tasks:

i) use technology and connectivity to share promising strategies, interesting case studies, and student and faculty learning opportunities that support program improvement.
ii) model, for program staff, effective uses of technology for professional productivity such as in presentations,

record keeping, data analysis, research, and communications.

iii) use online collaboration to build and participate in collaborative learning communities with directors of similar programs in other districts.

Technology opens up many doors for students at all academic levels to do real work as they study a particular subject. Integrating a curriculum with technology involves making technology into a tool to enhance learning in a content area or multidisciplinary setting. The technology should become an integral part of how the classroom functions, as accessible as all other classroom tools. Barriers to integration have included inadequate hardware and software, difficulties in securing sufficient funding, inadequate staff development, and deficiencies in planning.

A different sort of technology integration occurs with distance education. Offering courses with a remote teacher provides a school or district with an alternative way to extend the curriculum, and allows several districts to share a scarce or expensive resource. The number of distance education courses offered is an indication of the penetration of distance education into the school's instructional base.

Incorporation of desired technology proficiencies into standards for students and teachers is an indication of technology integration into the vision for the curriculum. Although such incorporation may not be the same as direct evidence of use, it denotes institutional incorporation of the technology goals. Institutional buy-in of this sort, backed with support from teachers and parents and administrators, is the way to guarantee that the adopted innovation will not disappear when circumstances change.

Instructional technology should prepare the student for lifelong learning in a rapidly changing technological society by providing a basic understanding of technology usage, processes and systems. This knowledge is necessary for all students regardless of educational or career goals. Each level of technology skill is built upon by previous levels. The skills addressed are:

i) operation of the computer
iii) application software as a tool
iv) problem-solving skills
v) telecommunications skills
vi) ethical and legal issues in technology

Technology-based student assessment types are follows:

i) multiple-choice test administered via computer;
ii) adaptive multiple-choice test;
iii) open-ended response test;
iv) electronic portfolio.

In all of these areas and more, there is a wealth of opportunities to communicate, and to gain in efficiency by more efficient communication. Computers support the organisation and efficient communication of information; the integration of technology into management involves, at its core, the promotion of efficiencies in sharing information.

Although these uses of technology may appear less glamorous than, say, allowing students to point a telescope remotely over the Internet, the potential effects of technology in school management are no less revolutionary than in other areas of enterprise management. Evaluations of integration will become easier and more commonplace with new software packages that enable schools to link vital data from almost all recordkeeping spheres into a cohesive and seamless database.

## TECHNOLOGY APPLICATIONS

The term technology applications refers to software and systems, run on school equipment, that support important administrative and instructional functions. The following functions represent the major categories of technology applications for schools:

i) *Administrative management software and systems:* Financial accounting; staff attendance and payroll; budgeting; operations and planning, including transportation and food systems; facilities management; inventory control; and decision support;

ii) *Instructional support software and systems:* Instructional planning and management, including grading, testing, and individualised educational program (IEP) management; instructional support, including student attendance; access to remote educational resources; and distance education.

iii) *Communications support:* Electronic mail; local-and wide-area networks; access to the Internet and remote educational and administrative sites; satellite uplinks and downlinks; and Internet-based telephony;

iv) *Operating systems; and Security systems:* Such as firewall technology, secure transmission systems, and antivirus software.

v) *Instructional application types:* Instructional process support; learning support (practice drills; problem solving; data analysis; simulation/demonstration; research; distance learning); assessment.

vi) *Teacher-support instructional applications :* Software or applications specifically designed to support teachers in instructional processes. Examples include attendance software; grading applications; testing systems; student work or portfolio systems; lesson planning software.

The basic tool skills that everyone involved in schools from the principal to the teacher to the student—must have in order to be able to use technology range from simple keyboarding to computer programming. While some skills obviously vary in complexity and may not be needed until higher education, basic capabilities have become part of a new literacy. Knowing them is akin to learning how to read in an earlier age: the mark of an educated, competent person.

Assessing the extent to which the school technology offerings teach these tool skills is very important and will no doubt become even more so as technology becomes more transparent in the classroom. As applications and devices in use in classrooms continue to evolve, and as technology becomes further integrated into education, what are considered "basic tool skills" can be expected to evolve.

There are a number of important communication functions that schools and districts carry out which technology can enable or improve. Communication between school staff and parents of students can be supported through class home-work assignment web pages or telephone hotlines. E-mail can support direct parent communication with teachers or the principal. Communication with the larger community is enabled by school web pages or online school "report cards"; the latter often become part of real estate agencies' electronic brochures for the community.

Schools use computer-based networks to conduct significant business with their districts, other institutions, and with state authorities. Data are sent to state education agencies; requests for purchases go back and forth from schools to central districts. Staff attendance records are forwarded to district payroll systems. Transcripts are sent to other schools or districts when students move, or to colleges when students graduate.

Standards for educational technology applications are being developed, with the potential to be used for assessment of instructional software and applications. Technical coordinators and other evaluators will have to develop criteria to evaluate the effectiveness of products beyond "best-of-breed" determinations. The situation is more problematic for evaluation of administrative software and applications. Standards for such applications do not exist or at least represent an entirely different framework.

Although information about technology applications is typically analysed at the school or district level, the relevant unit for data element definitions is the software program or application. Unit records for software form the basic elements for a comprehensive technology application database. A system based on unit records would meet day-to-day administrative needs and support overall assessment and planning.

## References

Barron, L. C., Goldman, E. S., "Integrating technology with teacher preparation", In B. Means (Ed.), *Technology and Education Reform* (pp. 57-81). San Francisco, CA: Jossey-Bass, 1994.

Becker, H., Ravitz, J. Wong, Y., "Teacher and teacher-directed student use of computers and software", *Report #3. Teaching Learning and Computing: 1998 National Survey*, Irvine, CA: University of California at Irvine, Center for Research in Information Technology in Organizations, 1999

Cuban, L., *Teachers and machines: The classroom uses of technology since 1920*, New York: Teachers College Press, 1986.

Harasim, L., "Online education: The future", In T. M. Harrison, & T. Stephen (Eds.), *Computer networking and scholarly communication in the twenty-first-century university*, New York: State University of New York Press, 1996.

Jonassen, D.H., *Computers in the classroom. Mindtools for critical thinking*", Englewood Cliffs, NJ: Prentice-Hall, 1996.

_______________ , "Evaluating constructivistic learning", In T. M. Duffy, D. H. Jonassen Eds, *Constructivism and the technology of instruction*, Hillsdale, NJ: Lawrence Erlbaum Associates Inc., 1992.

Ravitz, J., "Demystifying data about technology impacts in schools", Paper presented at the National Educational Computing Conference (NECC), San Antonio, TX, June, 2002.

_______________ , "After the wires: Implementation conditions related to increased teacher use of the Internet in schools with high Internet connectivity", Paper presented at Annual Meetings of the American Educational Research Association, Montreal, CA, April 1999.

_______________ , Becker, H, Wong, Y., "Constructivist Compatible Beliefs and Practices among U.S. Teachers", *Report #4. Teaching Learning and Computing: 1998*, Irvine, CA: University of California at Irvine, Center for Research in Information Technology in Organizations, 2000.

# 7

# Teaching in Early Childhood Education

There were two separate systems for the care and education of young children; full-day child care for children of working parents—usually low income children—and half-day nursery schools for middle and upper income children. Today, most early childhood educators agree that the care and education of young children should go hand-in-hand since both are needed if children are to develop and learn well. Programmes for young children are coming together; increasingly they have overlapping goals, use the same developmental knowledge base, similar pedagogical methods, and have increasingly integrated systems.

Children learn different things at different times, and new experiences must be within their zone of proximal development if they are to have an effect. Nevertheless, it is clear that early childhood is a time of rapid development and that deprivations and opportunities during this period can have long-term effects on children's learning. Children who have a broad base of experience in domain specific knowledge move more rapidly toward acquiring more complex skills. It seems that when children know something well, they can build on it to learn even more complex ideas. This new research has made it essential to reconsider many traditional beliefs about what young children can and cannot do or learn during their preschool years.

Children's brains are evidently pre-wired to encourage them to engage in social interchange, and infants are primed to gaze at their caregivers face. They respond to cuddling by calming down, and they seek out social interaction and will smile or look sad in response to the expression of their others. But, if no one provides attentive and responsive care, children's capacity to love and care about others doesn't develop. In addition, positive relationships predict later learning. Presumably this is because children attend better to objects that the caregiver shows interest in, are freer to explore when their caregiver is present, learn to control their feelings better when their caregiver is available, and are more willing to accept help from people they know and care about.

Adults, through their caregiving—by looking, touching, talking, feeding, changing clothes—by doing the ordinary things adults do, stimulate children's interest and learning. Through children's enjoyment of social relationships and through social mediation, children create their intelligence. The connection between children's relationships with their teachers is how well they learn in school. Children with positive relationships with their preschool teachers are more apt to learn better in kindergarten and children with good relationships with their kindergarten teachers learn to read faster.

During the preschool years, adults bring new experiences to children that challenge and excite them, thereby helping them learn. Children's experiences are defined by cultural definitions of appropriate goals and aspirations as well as by the kinds of experiences that are provided for them. Development and culture are two sides of the same coin, interacting to set parameters for individuals. Despite the fact that all children have learned a great deal before they come to school, all environments do not prepare children equally well for school.

For example, when children are exposed to environments that are rich in verbal language, they are apt to have greater ability to express ideas and learn to read than children who are exposed to more limited language environments are. Children learn what is in their environment to be learned and what they learn prepares them to learn more of similar things. While developmental competence may be similar across cultures, what children learn is, of course, different. If Spanish, Black English, or Chinese speaking and reading children must operate in an environment where only Standard English is used and they do not have a chance to learn it, then they are at a learning but not developmental disadvantage.

Culture becomes a problem when children are in environments that does not recognise the way their culture has taught them to express their developmental capabilities. Our world has changed and it is inevitable that what children need to know and be able to do has changed with it. As the global economy undermine the industrial focus of Americans industry, technology has moved to the forefront and the technological revolution is altering society as dramatically as did the industrial revolutions of the prior age.

Today, the mantra of business and government is that children who are not adequately educated cannot participate in the new economy and will become a drain on the society. Relationships between children and their teachers/caregivers are built on consistent and responsive interaction. Yet, assigned caregivers in infant programmes and looping are not widely practiced. Some teachers and caregivers have not thought of their work as a profession, a profession that requires continuing education to be informed about new research and reflection on practice to make good judgments about curricula.

During the preschool years, children have a literacy rich environment: with explicit opportunities to observe how literacy tools—paper, pencils, pens, technology—are used to create signs, write narratives, make lists, get information use computers, etc. Children should receive explicit alphabetic information, including the letter sound relationships. Early intervention programmes are developed to give children a leg up, to even the playing field, and they can have enormous consequence for their later educational achievement, but only if they are planned and carried out correctly.

The acquisition of both knowledge and skills is usually taken for granted as a goal for which educational institutions have a special, if not unique responsibility. That is not to say that knowledge and skills are not learned outside of schools. Families, museums, the media, libraries, sports clubs, and many other contexts are sources of voluntary as well as incidental knowledge and skill learning. However, schools and preschools are deliberately and explicitly designed to enhance knowledge and skill acquisition.

Most educators would also readily agree that many feelings (e.g., self-esteem) are influenced for better or worse by school experiences and are worthy of inclusion among curriculum goals. The terms inclinations, dispositions, and styles are used as subcategories of the variable "approaches to learning". These three terms appears in the indexes of major comprehensive child development texts.

The term cognitive style, frequently used in research on adults and children, has been defined as "ways that individuals perceive, think, understand, remember, judge, and solve problems", leaving no clear picture of what is not included in the definition, although cognitive styles represent important understandings of how learners respond to materials and communications.

The term learning style is increasingly linked to Howard Gardner's theory of multiple intelligences, in which distinctive strength or weakness in one or another of seven hypothesised types of intelligence is associated with a corresponding learning style. Many educators are attempting to apply this formulation of learning styles in curriculum and teaching practices. Assessment of the usefulness of learning styles associated with the theory of multiple intelligences seems premature at this time.

The formal definition suggests that the disposition construct is used to identify broad rather than specific categories of behaviour, or characteristic ways of responding to a variety of situations. A formal definition of dispositions as "summaries of act frequencies" that represent trends or frequencies of acts. According to this definition, a person exhibiting a relatively high frequency of behaviour such as making donations to charity, giving gifts to family members, and offering loans to needy friends, could be said to have the disposition to be generous. Similarly, children who frequently ask questions, often snoop and pry, and generally poke around their environment can be said to have a robust disposition to be curious.

The term disposition appears with increasing frequency in literature related to children's learning. According to J.C. Wakefield's definition, curiosity, generosity, and stubbornness could be classified as dispositions, and would not include capabilities like mastery of reading, arithmetic, or handwriting skills.

L.G. Katz suggests that the terms trait and disposition differ in at least two major ways. The first is that a disposition implies a trend in a person's actions rather than his or her emotional state. Thus terms like honesty, ambition, and courage do not fit a definition of a disposition, but describe aspects of a person's character and the management of his or her emotions. Disposition, on the other hand, can be used to designate actions and characterise their frequency.

An individual's dispositions can be implied by terms such as explorer, problem solver, bully, whiner, and so forth, which may however, be accompanied by emotional states. The term attitude has a long history of use among educators. In recent years, however, the meaning of the attitude construct has been the subject of substantial controversy. It is usually defined as "a relatively enduring organisation of beliefs around an object or situation predisposing one to respond in some preferential manner" to a given phenomenon, or as "an evaluative tendency that is expressed by evaluating a particular entity with some degree of favour or disfavour". In this sense, attitudes can be thought of as predispositions to act positively or negatively with respect to a particular phenomenon.

Although the shaping of attitudes is often listed among the goals of educational programmes (e.g., acquiring a positive attitude toward learning), the term attitude is not usually applied to preschool children, perhaps because they are assumed not to engage in evaluative thinking, but to respond momentarily in terms of largely spontaneous likes and dislikes, or to be somewhat *tabulae rasae* with respect to their larger environment.

Research on motivation related to dispositions comes under the rubric of mastery motivation. Several contrasts are offered by scholars studying this aspect of children's learning. Children oriented toward learning goals are interested in their own mastery for its own sake and those oriented toward performance goals are more concerned about others' judgments of their abilities. Learning-oriented children are more likely than performance-oriented children to believe that effort is effective, to vary their strategies in the face of difficulties, and to assist peers having difficulties.

An achievement goal concerns the purposes of achievement behaviour. It defines an integrated pattern of beliefs, attributions, and effect that produces the intentions of behaviour and that is represented by different ways of approaching, engaging in, and responding to achievement activities. With a mastery goal, individuals are oriented toward developing new skills, trying to understand their work, improving their level of competence, or achieving a sense of mastery based on self-referenced standards.

There are at least seven reasons for suggesting that dispositions should be included among the goals (each of which should be stated in terms of strengthening desirable and weakening undesirable dispositions) of early childhood education. The most important reason is that the acquisition of knowledge and skills alone does not guarantee that they will be used and applied. Second, dispositional considerations are important because the instructional processes by which some knowledge and skills are acquired may themselves damage or undermine the disposition to use them.

Third, some important dispositions relevant to education, such as the disposition to investigate, may be thought of as inborn. When children's experiences support the manifestations of a disposition with appropriate scaffolding and environmental conditions, it is likely to become robust and without such supportive experiences it is likely to weaken if not extinguish. Though knowledge and skills not acquired early in life might be acquired later, dispositions are probably less amenable to reacquisition once damaged or extinguished.

Fourth, the processes of selecting curriculum and teaching strategies should include considerations of how desirable dispositions can be strengthened and undesirable dispositions can be weakened. In the case of desirable dispositions, it seems reasonable to assume they are strengthened when an opportunity to manifest them is available, and vice versa for undesirable ones.

Fifth, on the basis of the evidence accumulated from research on mastery versus performance motivation, it seems reasonable to suggest that there is an optimum amount of positive feedback for young children above which children may become preoccupied with their performance and the judgments of others rather than involvement in the task, and hence their learning would be acquired at the expense of their disposition to learn. What constitutes an optimum level is likely to vary widely in any group of children, and must be determined by close observations of their reactions to adult feedback.

Sixth, dispositions are sufficiently important aspects of children's development and education to be among the goals, then they must be included in the evaluation and assessment of an educational programme. Inclusion of dispositions as goals requires determination of which dispositions to include and how their manifestation can be assessed.

Seventh, dispositions are not likely to be acquired through didactic processes, but are more likely modelled by young children as they experience being around people who exhibit them. Therefore, teachers and parents might consider what dispositions can be seen in them by the children they are responsible for. If teachers want their young pupils to have robust dispositions to investigate, hypothesize, experiment, conjecture, and so forth, they might consider making their own such intellectual dispositions more visible to the children.

## Early Childhood Education in Poor Communities

High-quality early childhood programmes, typically situated within centres or preschools, have demonstrated significant effects on early language and cognitive development for children from low income families. Yet, effects for similar children in "naturally" varying centres across poor communities are more mixed, likely because of wide variation in programme quality. Centre care for infants that manifests low quality may even depress early cognitive growth, relative to parental care. There is need for quality of care selected under the new policy regime by mothers moving from welfare to work.

Carefully crafted preschool programmes have shown significant effects repeatedly on young children's cognitive growth and, occasionally, on their social development. Generalising effects from these demonstration programmes to broadly available child care programs is difficult. Studies assessing the impact of centers—within both middle-class and low-income neighbourhoods—tends to show less consistent effects on young children's cognitive growth. In contrast to studies assessing child care type, studies looking at the influence of centre quality on children's outcomes tend to find effects.

Marked shifts in family policy over the past decade have influenced demand for child care and the mix of organisations and individuals that provide care in poor communities. The process of child care selection, the availability of home-based providers, and the quality of care may all be changing as welfare reforms become institutionalised, spurring greater demand for child care and sizable infusions of new funding.

Under strong and immediate pressure to work outside the home, low-income mothers may be constrained in their choices, depending on the stock of care options available locally. In this case, the mother's own attributes may have little effect on child care choice. If children are allocated into centre slots by caseworkers, traditional conceptions of demand factors operating solely at the individual level are not sufficient. In addition, state regulatory policies may affect the distribution of centre quality.

Alternatively, children exposed to risk factors at home may display a higher likelihood of being placed in home-based settings or in poorer quality centers, leading to selection bias when estimating discrete effects of nonparental child care. Evidence suggests that high-quality centre programs more effectively contribute to children's cognitive and language development than home-based providers.

## A Development Approach in Teaching Early Childhood Education

A developmental approach to curriculum and teaching methods is one that takes into account knowledge of human development and principles derived therefrom as they apply to decisions about curriculum content, teaching methods, and the developmental progression of learners. For providers of programs for young children, whether for a short or long day, major criteria for assessing the appropriateness of curriculum and pedagogical practices are based on what is assumed and what is known about the nature of development and the relationship between early experience and mature functioning.

A curriculum can be broadly defined as a plan for learning. For any age group, the curriculum is based explicitly and implicitly on assumptions about (a) what is worth learning, (b) how it is best learned, and (c) when it is best learned. A developmental approach to curriculum and teaching practices is one that addresses those aspects of learning that change with the age and experience of the learner.

A developmentally appropriate curriculum is one that is designed on the assumption that what children should learn, and the means by which they are most likely to learn it, change with their age and with the experience that accrues with age. In other words, in a developmental approach to curriculum design and teaching methods, answers to questions about what should be learned and how it would best be learned depend on what we know of the learner's developmental status. A developmental approach also depends on our understanding of the relationships between early experience and subsequent development and functioning.

The nature of development is only one possible criterion by which to judge the appropriateness of a curriculum or of teaching methods. A developmental approach takes into account two equally important dimensions of development: the normative and the dynamic dimensions. The normative dimension of development addresses the characteristics and capabilities of children that are typical or normal for their age group.

Age norms provide useful starting points for curriculum planning. Knowledge of age-typical interests and abilities can provide a basis for preliminary planning of a programme of activities and the selection of equipment and materials. Age norms are also useful for alerting teachers to individual children whose patterns of development depart noticeably from those of their age group and who warrant the kind of close observation necessary to ascertain whether special curriculum and teaching strategies are required.

The dynamic dimension of development deals with an individual child's progress from immaturity to maturity. Individual children change over time along this dimension. Their development reflects the long-term effects of early experience rather than the normality or typicality of behaviour and abilities of a particular age group. This dimension has three aspects: sequence, delayed effects, and cumulative effects.

*Sequence* refers to the order or stages of development through which an individual passes (e.g., from babbling to talking in achieving mastery of first language). Curriculum and teaching practices related to sequence consider what learning and developmental tasks have to be completed before the next learning is most likely to occur.

*Delayed effects* refer to the potential positive and negative effects of early experience that are not manifested at the time of occurrence but that influence later functioning (e.g., early infant-caregiver attachment may influence later parenting competence, a hypothesis that has been contentiously discussed among developmental psychologists for many years). This aspect of the dynamic dimension of development takes up issues concerning practices that are effective in the short term but may have delayed or "sleeper" effects that are deleterious in the long term (e.g., rewards and punishments or insecure early attachment of infants to caregivers). Similarly, some practices that may not seem important to development during the early years may have positive delayed effects later. Whether positive or negative, delayed effects are those effects that are not manifested until later in the course of development.

*Cumulative effects* refer to experiences that may have no observable effects (either positive or negative) if they occur occasionally or rarely but that may have powerful effects if they occur frequently (e.g., the cumulative positive effects of frequent block play or cumulative negative effects of frequent—even if mild-criticism).

All curriculum planners must take into account four categories of learning goals:

i) *Knowledge*: Knowledge includes facts, information, understandings, constructions, concepts, stories, songs, legends, and the like.
ii) *Skills*: Skills are relatively small units of action that can be easily observed and inferred from behaviour, including physical, social, and verbal skills of various levels of specificity.
iii) *Dispositions*: Dispositions are habits of mind—not mindless habits—with motivational and affective qualities that stimulate the manifestation of relevant behaviour, such as curiosity, cooperativeness, or quarrelsomeness and
iv) *Feelings*: Feelings are internal emotional states associated with most contexts and interactions

Some of the most important dispositions can be assumed to be inborn, such as the disposition to learn and to make sense of experience. Other dispositions are likely to be learned from being around people in whom both the desirable and undesirable ones can be seen. Furthermore, for dispositions to be strengthened, they must be manifested or expressed with a certain amount of frequency and experienced as satisfying and effective.

Thus, curriculum and teaching methods that provide contexts and opportunities for children to manifest desirable dispositions such as cooperation, conflict resolution, investigation, hypothesis-building, and the testing of hypotheses and predictions are developmentally appropriate.

Similarly, feelings are not learned from instruction or from exhortation. The capacities for some feelings, such as fear, anger, anxiety, and most likely joy as well, are probably inborn. But many feelings are learned from experience: feelings of belonging and of not belonging, feelings of competence and incompetence, feelings of confidence—high or low—and many other feelings of concern to families and educators are learned in the course of experiences provided in the educational setting.

### Principles of Developmental Approach

On the basis of the concept of development, and the assumptions derived therefrom concerning a developmental approach to planning for young children, the following principles of practice are offered.

*Principle 1*: A developmental approach to curriculum and teaching practices takes into account both the normative and dynamic dimensions of development, in that what young children should do and should learn is determined on the basis of what is best for their development in the long term rather than on simply what "works" in the short term. Taken together, the two dimensions of development suggest that just because children can do something (the normative dimension) does not mean that they should do it.

Young children can be coerced into learning and engaging in many activities that may not necessarily be in their best interests in the long term (the dynamic dimension), but that may seem acceptable, insignificant, or harmless in the short term. One example is the common use of tangible rewards such as prizes, certificates, and candies for correct performance on assigned tasks. There is good reason to believe that while such practices seem effective and even harmless in the short term, they may have negative consequences in the long term.

*Principle 2*: When young children are introduced to formal instruction too early, too intensely, and too abstractly, they may learn the knowledge and skills offered, but they may do so at the expense of the disposition to use them. For example, premature formal instruction in reading or arithmetic may succeed in equipping children with the intended skills and knowledge at a rudimentary level; however, the processes of learning through such instruction may damage their dispositions to become readers and users of the numeracy skills and concepts so painfully acquired.

The potential risk of premature formal instruction can be thought of as the damaged disposition hypothesis. This hypothesis may account for the common observation that children's natural dispositions to learn, explore, and investigate subside after a few years of schooling. This phenomenon is sometimes referred to as the second-grade "wash-out" phenomenon. The potential damage may not be apparent early in the children's school lives.

Most children during the early years are eager to please teachers and engage willingly in the activities provided for them. The damage is likely to be manifested as a cumulative effect of several years of excessive drill and practice of decontextualised skills that rely heavily on the practice of small bits of information and skills and rote memory. Thus, in curriculum planning, consideration is merited on the potential long-term cumulative effects of early experiences on the dispositions to apply what is learned.

*Principle 3*: Learning, especially in the early years, generally proceeds from behavioural knowledge to representational (or symbolic) knowledge. By way of example, the distinction between behavioural and representational knowledge can be seen in language development. Namely, preschoolers have the behavioural knowledge that enables them to use their mother tongue long before they can represent it in the form of abstract grammatical categories such as nouns and verbs.

Similarly, young children can navigate their homes and immediate neighbourhoods correctly long before they can represent them in the form of maps or directional concepts such as right and left or east and west. A developmentally appropriate curriculum is one that broadens and deepens children's behavioural knowledge by providing a variety of first-hand experiences. That helps young children represent their experiences through a wide variety of media, including verbal expression, literary and graphic languages, models, and dramatic play. In the processes of representing their understandings, children can be guided by adults so that their understandings of what they already know become deeper, fuller, more accurate, and more finely differentiated.

*Principle 4*: Unless children have some experience of what it feels like to understand some topics in depth, their disposition to seek indepth understandings cannot be developed and strengthened. Many curriculum and pedagogical practices in early childhood and elementary education emphasise superficial acquaintance with information and "smatterings" of knowledge of many things, rather than the acquisition and construction of indepth understandings of phenomena worthy of an investment of the children's time and energy.

Indeed, one of the issues that deserves more discussion than it currently receives is the overcrowding of the early childhood and primary school curriculum. This overcrowding can lead to fragmentation and excessive emphasis on coverage versus mastery of disparate knowledge and skills. Yet the disposition to seek indepth understanding of complex phenomena worthy of children's and adults' attention is essential for competent participation in democratic processes and thus one of the important ultimate goals of education in this country.

*Principle 5*: When young children are frequently coerced into behaving as though they understand something well, when they really do not (e.g., premature instruction in the calendar or in formal arithmetic), confidence in their own intellects, observations, hypotheses, and questions may be undermined, and in some cases may be abandoned. The cumulative effect on young children of repeated experience in situations in which they must act without real or confident understanding may be a weakening or distrust of their natural dispositions to construct their own understandings of their experiences. This cumulative effect may undermine their motivation to learn.

*Principle 6*: For young children, investigation and observation are ways of learning as natural as play. Early childhood specialists and practitioners have a long tradition of asserting that play is the natural way that young children learn. Indeed, all young mammals play spontaneously and, in their play, rehearse behaviour they will use in their maturity. Experience of living and working with young children easily strengthens our appreciation of the basis of this traditional emphasis on the educational value of play—one that may have developed at a time when children's play was not valued and when few play materials were available for young children.

Nevertheless, this tradition should not diminish acknowledgment that it is just as natural for children to learn through direct observation and investigation as through play. Adults can readily see the very young observe phenomena around them with great interest. Similarly, from infancy onward, children put enormous amounts of time and energy into investigating their physical and social environments—often exposing themselves to danger in the process.

Young children are natural anthropologists, linguists, and scientists. Most children naturally and spontaneously generate explanations and hypotheses to account for what they observe, whether the phenomenon in question is rain, worms, or cashiers in the supermarket. Their conjectures can be followed up with close observations, interviews, and other fact-finding activities through which their predictions and hypotheses can be tested.

In other words, a child-sensitive and developmentally appropriate curriculum is one that capitalises on children's natural impulse to find out what the objects around them are made of, how they work, where they come from, what they are used for, what they are called, what the people around them do, when and why they do what they do, and so forth. A curriculum for young children that takes into account the nature of their development is one that addresses their natural dispositions to observe and investigate their surroundings.

*Principle 7*: The goal of all education is to engage the mind of the learner in its fullest sense, including its aesthetic, moral, social, and spiritual sensibilities. Enjoyment is not a main goal of education; it is a main goal of entertainment. The ultimate goal of all education at every level is to engage the mind so as to strengthen the learner's disposition to go on learning. Curriculum and teaching strategies that succeed in fully engaging children's minds provide experiences that are enjoyable; but enjoyment is not the goal of such experiences.

*Principle 8*: Children's dispositions to be interested, engaged, absorbed, and involved in intellectual effort are strengthened when they have ample opportunity to work on a topic or investigation over extended periods of time. The term interest refers to the capacity to "lose oneself" in something outside of oneself and to sustain the effort of pursuing ideas and completing tasks through even their routine elements.

A curriculum characterised by a succession of brief one-shot activities completed in a few minutes and not resumed for further development may weaken children's dispositions to explore topics indepth, to reach for fuller and deeper understanding, and to become absorbed in worthwhile pursuits. Children in contemporary society have little opportunity to appreciate the length of time and the amount of effort required for the most important basic elements in their lives.

*Principle 9*: When young children's interests draw them to real events, particularly those in which adults are involved, and the adults respond to this interest by providing support and information, by focusing children's attention on important aspects of the phenomenon of interest, and by inviting their participation in the activity, the children are in an optimal environment. Young children—especially in the toddler years—are often attracted to real events in their environment (e.g., an adult who is cooking, repairing a household item, cleaning the furnace, or building a fence).

When the adult involved responds to that interest with information and suggestions for how the child can participate, or provides simple reasons why she or he cannot participate in some parts of the activity, or gives information in response to the child's questions and appreciates the elements the child shows interest in, the child is in an optimal learning environment and is learning as an apprentice. Such learning can only occur if something real and intriguing to the child is in progress in his or her presence. Such real and actual events can be part of good project work. If few real events or tasks are available in the classroom, teachers are obliged to find other ways to motivate children. When a teacher, for example, is arranging the classroom environment so that it will be hospitable to a small animal, the children can be drawn into the process and adopt the teacher's concerns and interest in the task.

When the teacher presents children with tasks for the children's benefit only and of no real interest to the teacher, she may have to resort to high praise, coercion, or cajoling to get the children involved. While not all tasks involved in the mastery of basic literacy and numeracy can be equally interesting, a balance of systematic skill instruction, interesting project work, and spontaneous play is most likely to support children's dispositions to learn and their general growth and development.

*Principle 10*: Desirable dispositions are not likely to be learned from instruction; rather, they are learned from being around significant others who exhibit, exemplify, and model them. To return to the matter of dispositional goals, for dispositions to be strengthened, they must be manifested effectively and appreciated (i.e., responded to appropriately, rather than rewarded). As already suggested, desirable and undesirable dispositions are learned also from models and are strengthened by being manifested and effective.

Research indicates that excessive use of rewards, prizes, certificates, stickers, and trophies may undermine and weaken the development of intrinsic motivation, that is, the disposition called interest. A curriculum that includes involving children in investigation projects provides contexts in which intrinsic motivation and interest can be manifested, satisfied, appreciated, and thereby strengthened.

*Principle 11*: Feelings are not likely to be learned through instruction; both desirable and undesirable feelings are learned in the context of and as consequences of experience. Feelings of confidence and self-esteem, for example, are not likely to be strengthened from instruction, exhortation, incantation, or admonition, but they arise indirectly as the consequences of experiences that have other goals. Similarly, feelings of low self-esteem and anxiety, for example, are not likely to be alleviated by exhortation or empty flattery.

Children are most likely to acquire self-esteem when adults esteem them. This means that children are treated respectfully as people—though young ones-with minds, ideas, thoughts, hypotheses, interests, and real concerns. Thus, when appropriate investigative project work is included in the curriculum, children have ample opportunity to make decisions, to assist each other, to argue about their ideas and plans, and to take initiative and responsibility for the work they accomplish.

*Principle 12*: Young children should be engaged daily in worthwhile activities and work in which their cooperation is functional and not phony. This principle implies that children should be engaged frequently and regularly in group work in which each participant has the opportunity to make individual contributions to the total effort and to take a part of the responsibility for the accomplishment of the group's goals.

*Principle 13*: The younger the learners, the more important is the goal to strengthen their disposition to look more closely at phenomena and events in their own environments worth learning more about. This principle addresses the content of the curriculum of which a major goal is to strengthen children's inborn disposition to make sense of their experiences and environments. A major responsibility of teachers of young children is to alert them to phenomena and events in their own environments and experiences worthy of their attention and deeper understanding. As children grow older and gain a firm grasp of their own experience and environment, it is the responsibility of educators to strengthen children's dispositions to make sense of other people's experiences and environments—those that are distant in both time and place.

*Principle 14*: The younger the learners, the more important it is that what they are learning about (knowledge) and what they are learning to do (skills) have horizontal rather than vertical relevance. Horizontal relevance means that the knowledge and skills to be learned are meaningful and useful at the time they are learned. Vertical relevance refers to learning of knowledge and skills that are intended and expected to be meaningful and useful at some point in the future and that are designed to prepare the learner for the next grade, the next school . . . the next life! As children grow older, their capacity to benefit from knowledge and skills that have vertical rather than horizontal relevance most likely increases. Furthermore, as children grow older they are more able to understand and accept the reasons for mastering knowledge and skills that will have relevance and value for future experiences.

During the early years, excessive emphasis on knowledge and skills that have vertical rather than horizontal relevance may not only undermine children's dispositions to learn but also their confidence in their own intellectual powers. Many teachers complain that they are required to instruct children in knowledge and skills for which they believe them to be unready. However, they say that if they fail to do so, the teacher of the next grade will complain.

*Principle 15*: The younger the learners, the more they learn through interactive rather than reactive and receptive experiences, through direct and first-hand experiences rather than indirect and second-hand experiences, and through active rather than passive experiences. As children grow older, their capacities to benefit from passive learning, from indirect and second-hand learning, increase. While young children do learn from passive experiences (e.g., from stories, movies, or television), the major intellectual dispositions, such as to inquire, hypothesize, explore, experiment, investigate, analyse, and synthesise, are strengthened in the early years primarily through interactive experiences.

*Principle 16*: The younger the learners, the more important it is that they have ample opportunity to interact with real objects and real environments. When young children are obliged to "acquire" or assimilate knowledge about things that are not real-or at least very vivid to them-they are likely to have difficulty in contributing ideas, hypotheses, predictions, and information, or to pose meaningful questions to be answered through investigation, exploration, observation, discussion, and argument.

When the topics introduced to young children are too remote from their own first-hand experience, their dependence on the teacher for ideas and information is increased. Young children are dependent upon adults for many of the most important aspects of their lives; however, excessive and unnecessary dependence on adults in learning situations may undermine the development of their intellectual dispositions.

*Principle 17*: The younger the learners, the more important it is that they have opportunities to apply in meaningful contexts the knowledge and skills learned in the more formal parts of the curriculum. Good project work in which children investigate events and phenomena in their environments worth learning more about, and represent the results of their investigation, provides meaningful contexts for children to apply the skills taught in the more formal parts of the curriculum. Indeed, involvement in project investigations often motivates children to seek help from teachers and others in strengthening their formal literacy and numeracy skills to use in representing their observations and findings.

*Principle 18*: The younger the learners, the wider the variety of pedagogical approaches and methods that must be used. When a single method of teaching is used with a group of children that is diverse in background, development, experience, interests, abilities, and aptitudes, a significant proportion of the group is likely to fail. When using a single method for teaching a whole class, the chances are that about a third of the children already know what is being taught, about a third will learn it, and the remaining third will be unlikely to grasp it; in this way, whole-group instruction means that two-thirds of the children may be wasting their time!

*Principle 19*: The younger the learner, the larger the role of adults in helping them to develop social competence. Children who fail to achieve at least minimal social competence by about the age of six are at significant risk for school failure, later mental health difficulties, and dropping out of school. As children grow older, the problems of overcoming social difficulties increase. Children's social competence can be strengthened, in the presence of adults prepared to assist them, through participation in activities requiring social understanding and social interactive skills.

## References

Barnett, W. S., "Long-term effects of early childhood programs on cognitive and school outcomes", *Future of Children*, 5(3), 25 - 50, 1995.

Bee, H., *The Developing Child, Fourth Edition*, New York: Harper and Row, 1985.

Corno, L., "Encouraging Students to Take Responsibility for Learning and Performance", *The Elementary School Journal* 93(1): 69-84, 1992.

Ennis, R.H., "A Taxonomy of Critical Thinking Dispositions and Abilities", In J.B. Baron and R.S. Sternberg, Eds, *Teaching Thinking Skills: Theory and Practice*, Hillsdale, NJ: Lawrence Erlbaum Associates, 1987

Bowman, B., "Kindergarten practices for children from low income homes", In R. Pianta & M. Cox, Eds., *The transition to kindergarten*, Baltimore, MD: Paul H. Brookes, 1999.

Howes, C., Phillips D, Whitebook, M., "Thresholds of quality: implications for the social development of children in center-based child care", *Child Development, 63,* 449 - 460, 1992.

Katz, L.G., "Dispositions in Early Childhood Education" *ERIC/ EECE, Bulletin* 18(2): 1-3, 1985.

_______________ "Early Education: What Should Young Children Be Doing?" In S.L. Kagan and E.F. Zigler Eds, *Early Schooling: The National Debate*, New Haven: Yale University Press. pp. 151-167, 1987.

Pianta, R. and Cox, M., Eds., *Transition to kindergarten*, Baltimore, MD: Brookes Publishing Co., 1999.

Powell, D., *Strengthening parental contributions to school readiness,* Washington, DC: U.S. Department of Education, Office of Educational Research and Improvement, 1991.

Shonkoff, J, Phillips, D., *From neurons to neighborhoods: The science of early childhood development,* Washington, DC: National Academy Press, 2000.

Shipman, S.L., "Limitations of Applying Cognitive Styles to Early Childhood Education", *Early Child Development and Care* (51): 13-28, 1989.

Snow, C.E., Burns, M.S, Griffin, P., Eds. *Preventing reading difficulties in young children*, Washington, DC: National Academy Press, 1998.

# 8

# Teaching in Higher Education

Defining learning objectives requires teachers to make conscious choices about a wide range of teaching and learning considerations. The process of identifying teaching/learning objectives essentially defines what it is the teacher wants the student to learn. The focus of this planning is on the inputs to the learning experience and can be described as teacher-centred. For educators who subscribe to a learner-centred pedagogy, learning objectives are less acceptable than the notion of learning outcomes. The expectations for writing learning objectives include defining:

i) who is to perform the desired behaviour (e.g., the student);

ii) what the actual behaviour would be to demonstrate the objective

iii) result of the behaviour (e.g., the product)

iv) conditions under which the behaviour would be performed; and

v) standard used to evaluate the success of the product.

Better learning outcomes are less prescriptive and are meant to facilitate the student's orientation to the subject being studied as well as guiding the choice of teaching/learning/assessment strategies for the course/module. They are meant to communicate course/module expectations to the student, so they should be stated in a language that the student would understand. It is not uncommon when reading the literature on organising learning in higher education to find the terms 'objectives' and 'outcomes' used interchangeably or together, as objectives/outcomes.

The distinctions are frequently overlooked because, despite the variations in how they have been defined, when used, both require greater explicitness and transparency with regard to planning the teaching/learning process. When asked how they go about planning, academics often identify a process described as the 'intellectual approach'. That is, they start by listing topics they wish to cover in a course/module, placing primary emphasis on disciplinary content. Subject specialists in the arts and humanities often report using the 'experiential approach' to planning and those in the physical sciences and medicine tend to report using a 'problem-based approach'. Others may use a combination of approaches when planning courses.

Knowledge of the various approaches to learning design is useful when reviewing and assessing teaching practice. There are five approaches to course/module design: systematic, intellectual, problem-based, creative/experimental and training/workshop-based.

*Systematic*: Proceeds from identifiable needs to predictable outcomes. It follows a planning sequence with a feedback loop for changing and improving the design each time the course is taught.

*Intellectual*: Examines the subject matter in terms of assumptions held in the discipline with regard to a particular body of information, attitudes and skills. It asks questions such as: should the course be taught at the macro- or micro-level of conceptual analysis?

*Problem-based*: Identifies one or more specific problems to be addressed. It is not objective-defined but objective-based through inference. It eventually gets to a systematic approach but not sequentially. It places an emphasis on the process of understanding the problem.

*Creative/experiential*: Involves teaching/learning by experience and generally through the dynamics of a group process. Outcomes are defined in the existential moment of learning.

*Training/workshop-based*: Outcomes are defined by the skills acquired through the training workshop.

These approaches are commonly used in higher education. The systematic approach to course/module planning is most closely linked to the outcomes approach to teaching and learning. In fact, the specification of outcomes is the first step in the systematic approach. Integral to this approach is the interrelationship of the various steps, i.e., each part links to and informs the others in an interactive fashion.

Recently four 'domains' of intended learning outcomes for programmes of study in higher education in the United Kingdom have been proposed: knowledge and understanding; key skills: communication, numeracy, IT, learning to learn; cognitive skills (e.g., ability in critical analysis) and subject specific skills (e.g., laboratory skills). For some disciplines and in some universities, specification based on these four 'domains' would present no problem because the current practice is not dissimilar. For others this would mean radical change and would raise issues of acceptability in relation to the teaching of discipline.

Understanding the domains of learning, whatever the classification, is the first step in establishing levels of learning outcomes, but more important are the levels themselves. Research on deep and surface approaches to learning has also influenced thinking on levels of outcomes and views all learning as having five levels delineated as: an increase in knowledge, memorising, the acquisition of procedures, the abstraction of meaning, and understanding reality. When the teaching and learning outcomes focus on the first three levels, this is called a 'surface' approach to learning. When they focus on the last two levels, this is called a 'deep' approach to learning. The major difference between the two types of learning are the levels of meaning placed by the student on knowledge acquisition.

The systematic approach to organising teaching and learning is to identify the major categories of student characteristics that affect the learning experience of students. Some of the characteristics that have been found useful to the planning process include: knowledge on entry, personal characteristics, demographics, variables and learning style. Once identified, a match can be made between student needs and learning outcomes. For example, knowledge on entry will clearly help determine the topics to be examined and the depth of their consideration in a course/module. If getting information on the students for your specific course is difficult, aggregate information on students at the institution can prove quite useful. Some institutions are well equipped to provide a wide range of information on students enrolled on specific programmes; others are not. In a systematic approach to course/module planning, designing the teaching and learning units, choosing and implementing teaching and learning strategies, and assessing the teaching and learning are the critical steps which need to be directly linked to the outcomes planned. There is no correct teaching and learning strategy and there may be many possible routes to this end. The systematic approach also includes a revision cycle. This is meant to allow for the improvement of the course/module delivery and achievements of students' learning.

Many students seriously struggle at university. Though there is some evidence that universities seem to be thinking more about how to induct new students into university study, there is no consistency across universities. The impression given is that the university believes that they should be thrown in the deep end and left to get on with it. Now this may suit certain students, but as universities are opening their doors to more and more students, there will be an increasing amount of students who will not be able to cope with this approach.

While students value the independence of university study, teachers must be aware that becoming an independent learner does not happen overnight and that many students will need help in developing the appropriate skills. The key issue here is what is the university doing to help them. If this help appears not to be available, then this further reinforces the message is that teaching is not a priority.

The university teachers do not have to undergo any training as they are considered qualified by virtue of their academic credentials. Trainee teachers have to go through an intensive training year before they are permitted to have the responsibility for educating the nation's young people. Teachers are constantly being assessed on whether or not they are meeting the objectives. The obvious way of doing that is exam results, but the assessment process goes on all the time.

## Teaching Practice in Higher Education

Student expectations of tutors are much lower in higher education. There is not the inbuilt culture within the institution where tutors are reflecting on whether their students are actually learning and what they could do to improve their own teaching. The current situation tends to place the 'ball' of responsibility for learning totally in the students' court. If a student doesn't understand a lecture, can't take notes, doesn't understand a reading, doesn't speak in seminar or writes a bad essay, there is rarely a discussion of changing anything the tutor does.

Now many tutors do question themselves and make changes—many postgraduate tutors do this regularly. However, it is not the expectation of everyone. It all depends on the particular tutor. If someone is publishing regularly and bringing in research grant money, there would be no question of highlighting any lack of teaching ability. It is true that the current system is fostering a situation where teachers are spoonfeeding the students in order to ensure that their pass rate is high.

Another key difference is a lack of explicitness over the actual objectives of teaching. This is an important issue for postgraduate teachers. The following suggestions are improving teaching and learning:

i) Discussion within departments about what the actual objectives of the teaching are. There should be a collective approach where the department has worked out the kind of knowledge and skills and capacities they would like the students to develop.

ii) The different courses need to reinforce each other in the achievement of these objectives. For example, the department might identify key ideas that they want the students to have knowledge of or skills in. They then need to decide in which year to introduce these ideas. They may decide that there should be a progression such that certain ideas are introduced in the first year and then developed in the next two. The same is true of skills. What are the expectations of the students over the course of the three years?

iii) The above process will require an awareness of differences between students. Some students may achieve the goals for the third year in the first year, so there needs to be room for differentiation. Also, if one of the objectives is for students to become independent and self-directed learners then there must be scope for this development, providing increasing amounts of opportunities to do so as they progress in their studies.

iv) The whole process has to be monitored. Students' progress needs to be kept track of, not just in terms of exam marks or essay marks that are just left in the file.

v) Once tutors are clear about what the objectives are, then it will become easier to plan the teaching. They may even decide that the lecture/seminar format is not the most effective. Or they may devise different forms of assessment. This can only be done, though, once tutors know what the goal is.

vi) The students need to be made aware of the objectives and the expectations teachers have of them. This will help put a stop to the tendency of the students thinking that they can get away with not attending or not doing much work. It would be impossible for learning strategies to work if the students are only there half of the time. Clear objectives and expectations would also help reduce the tendency of giving good reports to tutors who don't make them do anything or just have a good personality. They will learn to appreciate different tutors as long as they realise that the tutor is trying to help them achieve certain objectives. Tutors have different styles and personalities which are impossible to change. Teaching should not be a popularity contest.

vii) The broad objectives need to be translated into manageable parts. So if one of the objectives is very broad, like getting the students to have a working understanding of the main theoretical approaches in anthropology, then that needs to be broken down. The same with skills. If the objective is to enable students to understand and use a wide variety of readings, then strategies have to be adopted over a number of courses. Each course and each lesson will have its own role to play in achieving the overall aims and objectives.

viii) It will be impossible for tutors to implement the objectives if they have no training. There are two models of training: the tutor is left to work things out independently with informal advice from colleagues or the college-wide skills based approach where the institution runs a few generic courses that are supposed to add to the tutor's skills. But training has to be more than that. In addition, it needs to be subject specific or much of what is done will seem to be irrelevant.

A focus on teaching and learning should not mean more paper work, bureaucratic procedures and stressful assessments. If training and professionalisation do get forced on university departments from the top, with 'experts' coming in and evaluating and assessing and requiring evidence and quantitative measurements, it could be a disaster. It will kill any real reflection.

## Advances in Teacher Assessments

Technology is greatly increasing students' ability to understand and learn complex material; it is inspiring revolutionary changes in classrooms, schools, and the entire school system. The outcome for technology use that would be most valued by educators and parents alike is cognitive gains for students. If students are shown to have increased skills, abilities, performance, or thought processes associated with future success, the innovative educational practice will be judged successful.

Evaluations are more likely to look at whether students have specific knowledge (standardised tests) than whether students have acquired higher-order thinking and problem-solving skills that would allow them to gain and apply knowledge effectively in the future. Evaluations are more likely to look at whether teachers have mastered specific technology skills than to what extent they can affectively apply those skills to enhancing teaching and learning.

To win acceptance, educational technology is often promoted using an efficiency argument: technology will help students master the traditional goals of schooling. These are the goals being measured in existing standardised tests. But technology's strength is often seen in new possibilities for learning, e.g., using simulations to build inferential skills.

Learners' cognitive growth is of central interest when evaluating innovative educational programmes. If students are shown to have increased skills, abilities, performance levels, or thought processes associated with future success, the innovation is judged favourably. Even when students are not the primary target of the innovation, the project is often justified by the contribution it will ultimately make to student learning.

Basic-skills tests of academic achievement are also commonly used at the state and local levels as measures of school or teacher performance. In particular, the areas of academic achievement, critical thinking, problem solving, creativity, knowledge transfer, and skill acquisition are addressed. In addition to a brief clarification of each topic, methodological strategies appropriate for the design of learner cognition measures are described.

Methodologies available for assessment in the cognitive domains vary widely, with each approach providing a benefit to the overall understanding of the learner. Direct approximations of academic achievement are available from standardised measures, tailored tests, and various alternative assessment methods. Standardised tests of achievement that are used at the local and state level are generally written for basic-skills content and are primarily used to indicate proficiency at a particular grade or skill level.

One methodological concern with using school or district-mandated, group-administered standardised tests is the variability in administration. Teachers have been observed to vary the methods of test administration enough to significantly influence groups' scores on high-stakes tests of achievement. Teacher behaviours that influence student scores include providing additional instructions, rewording instructions for clarity, and answering questions that arise during the test period.

These variations are generally dismissed as measurement error, but support the preference for using individually administered achievement tests by trained psychometricians when feasible. Naturally, the use of a research design that establishes two groups who receive differing levels of exposure to the primary independent variable allows for more confidence when percentiles, raw scores, or stanine scores from archival records are the only measures available. In the case of percentile and raw scores, it is advantageous to transform to a scale score that is universal with respect to standard deviation

Tests that are developed to assess the specific goals of an intervention are referred to as tailored tests. Many educational technology projects use a tailored outcome measure because available standardised tests do not match the goals of the project. Either they do not measure valued goals of the project, or they measure too many goals in addition to those that the project is trying to affect. Often, tailored tests are not as psychometrically sound as standardised measures, because less time and effort is invested at the development stage to refine the pool of items. However, tailored tests can provide compelling evidence when the tests meet basic standards of reliability, validity, and scale construction.

Academic achievement estimates can be obtained through authentic assessments as an alternative to standardised tests, typically providing a more context-dependent rating of achievement. Authentic assessment methods typically involve direct examination of work quality through project-based learning, observing performance in a structured setting or presentation, or evaluating work products contained in a portfolio. One alternative strategy to measuring academic achievement relies on systematic observations of student responses to educational or learning antecedents.

This approach requires more indepth analyses of individual learners (thereby limiting sample sizes in most cases), but has an advantage in the standard unit of measure for learning, which is an observable and quantifiable event.

The use of structured observations by trained evaluators in a classroom setting may also be considered a form of direct approximation of student achievement. As with observations of any behaviour, measuring achievement or performance is most effective when the observation goals are clear, observers are trained to a criterion of acceptable performance, and the evaluator has a checklist or scoring protocol to work with during the observation.

Indirect approximations of learner achievement are estimations of performance level provided by significant others or by records maintained on ratings of achievement. A distinction between grades and performances on achievement measures is made here, as there are generally multiple factors affecting the assignment of a grade by a teacher. Grades are often a combination of measured academic performance coupled with judgments about performance potential, personal potential, or any one of a myriad of social factors.

Teacher ratings of student performance can be gathered through interviews, questionnaires, or archival searches of grade reports or portfolio comments. The more specific the estimate of performance the teacher provides, the closer the rating is likely to be to the learner's actual achievement. Naturally, the use of teacher ratings adds another dimension of measurement error in the evaluation. Parents can also provide estimates of their child's performance. The selection of parents over teachers should be viewed with caution, but is appropriate under select circumstances.

Parents are better judges of young children's ability levels during preschool years, provided the parents are asked to indicate ability or skill in specific domains and activities. Parents can be more reliable than teachers when the teacher has limited experience with students—for example, at the beginning of a school year. The use of both parents' and teachers' ratings of children's ability or performance levels can enhance the accuracy and quality of performance data.

Higher-order cognitive processes generally refer to the wide array of human cognitive activity that goes beyond rote memory and repetition. Evaluations of higher-order processes are often driven by an attempt to characterise learners' cognitive representations of knowledge or learning strategies. The importance of examining data other than achievement measures rests in the theoretical significance of the learning-performance differential.

The distinction between learning and performance rests on the fact that all achievement tests are imperfect measures of learning and are thus limited in scope and utility. Thus, there is generally a concern that achievement tests miss the benefits gained in projects that target the development of thinking strategies or skills. The inferential extensions made in analyses of higher-order cognition are indeed large, and require well-established theoretical rationales prior to making determinations regarding programme efficacy.

The strategies for evaluating problem solving and critical thinking skills are complementary cognitive activities, and the procedures for detecting ability or growth in these two domains of thinking are often similar, critical thinking and problem solving are distinct constructs. Critical thinking is one of many cognitive constructs that are ill-defined, or more precisely, differentially defined by researchers from various disciplines and research orientations.

The focus on critical thinking in the past two decades derives largely from the judgment by researchers and educators that too many educated individuals were incapable of engaging in critical thought, and a belief that critical thinking skills are necessary for success in modern society. When learners are shown to have heightened skills in critical thinking, and are able to engage in those processes independently, there is heightened expectation the learner will enjoy pronounced success in academic settings, and will likely develop lifelong learning practices and skills.

Whereas the identification of critical thinking generally involves the affective component of attitude, the broad category of cognitive processes referred to simply as "problem solving" is limited primarily to the exhibitions of a combination of skills. The following are the six steps that are inherent in most problem solving activities, including:

i) Recognition of the problem
ii) Definition of the problem
iii) Generation of strategies for solving the problem
iv) Accurate representation of relevant information
v) Allocation of resources for problem resolution
vi) Self-monitoring and evaluation of outcomes.

Problem solving models may also incorporate steps that involve the identification of goals in the problem situation, and an intermediate evaluation of the likelihood of success for generated strategies. The trend to promote project-based learning or guided discovery approaches to instruction has heightened the attention to problem solving skills and critical thinking.

The combination of problem solving and critical thinking strongly resembles the goals of inquiry-based learning strategies, where learners work to answer real-world problems and develop more advanced knowledge bases through their attempts to explain unintuitive results and conditions.

Effective evaluation of higher-order cognitive skills fostered in these inquiry-based learning activities can be facilitated through the acquisition of learning artifacts and sample discourse that demonstrate learner performance in context. There are several standardised performance measures available for both group and individual administration. These performance-based tasks provide the learner with a series of problem types or questions that require higher-order cognitive strategies for accurate completion.

The use of tailored measures of problem solving and critical thinking can be a sensible approach to measuring higher-order cognition, but must be firmly grounded in theory. This is usually attained through task analysis for each set of items and determining the processes most likely to underlie a variety of conclusions or solutions that may be derived in response to the task. Again, artifacts from contextually relevant problem-solving situations are useful materials for making determinations of higher-order cognitive processing, provided the activity leading to the artifact was well-structured.

Technology tools are becoming routinely utilised to gather data on higher-order cognition. Particularly effective methods of gaining insight into learners' cognitive processes, learning styles, and problem solving strategies involve the unobtrusive gathering of real-time data as students work through problems or learning materials. An alternate strategy for direct approximations of critical thinking and problem solving involves the process of dynamic assessment. This approach deviates from static assessment practices by allowing the test administrator to interact with the learner during the assessment period.

The test administrator may provide directive feedback or utilise mediational strategies that more directly mimic the learning and performance activities common to educational settings. The common static assessment procedures do not allow for interaction between the learner and the test administrator primarily in order to provide testing situations that are identical across settings. However, the use of dynamic assessment strategies has been suggested to provide more accurate estimates of ability for learners who are misrepresented with static assessment tools, including young children, learners with language, developmental, or learning deficits, and children from diverse cultural backgrounds.

Self-report ratings of higher order cognitive processes are also feasible, but are generally more effective when the learner provides ratings on distinct skills and abilities, rather than attempting to provide general ratings. Self-reported values are not realistic in young children, as they are not likely to possess the metacognitive awareness or self-appraisal skills needed to provide accurate estimations. There is little agreement among scholars regarding what constitutes creativity. One attempt stresses that creativity is demonstrated in products or responses that are novel, valuable, and heuristic in nature. The creativity consists of at least four components:

i) environmental factors that promote creativity,
ii) personality characteristics that predict creativity,
iii) the production of creative works, and
iv) the process of creative thought or action.

Promoting creativity in itself may not be as universally valued as boosting test scores, but creative thought is a beneficial cognitive tool for learners to develop and exhibit. The assessment of creativity is tricky, and subject to criticism as there is no standard scale of creativity, and developmental issues impact the level of creativity being exhibited.

Research in the area of creativity has produced varying scales, measures, and methodologies that have attempted to capture the essence of the ability and propensity to produce creative works. Unfortunately, it has been demonstrated that the method of measurement significantly impacts the resultant creativity rating. Direct approximations of creativity can involve the examination of life accomplishments and activities, or the use of an established measure of creativity (e.g., tests of divergent thinking). The relationships between these various strategies generally suggest that established-scales of creativity are reasonable predictors of lifelong creative productivity.

The shift toward problem-based learning has provided a wealth of finished materials in many educational settings. However, to evaluate creativity in a project, it is necessary to first know the nature of the assigned project. Identical work products can have varying levels of exhibited creativity, depending upon the parameters of the original task assignment. The creation of a computer simulation for a recently read story can be a very creative solution for an assigned book report, but may simply be fulfilling the requirements of an assignment when a teacher specifies the medium and content of delivery.

One effective way to evaluate creativity through archival work products is to evaluate several pieces of an individual's work to demonstrate a pattern of creativity. Alternatively, creativity can be assessed through consensus of a group of judges who work independently to assess the creative merits of artifacts by drawing from their expertise in the domain. The most common methods of indirect approximations of creativity are through ratings provided by significant others or self-reports of creative activity.

Self-reports of creativity are indirect approximations due to the unavailability of the actual creative products or processes for evaluation. However, this approach to developing ratings of creativity addresses the creative person, and identifies those individuals who have produced creative works in various domains and genres. This method of gathering creativity estimations is perhaps the most suspect with respect to inaccurate estimations of what is creative, but can provide an added dimension for creativity when combined with a direct approximation or significant others' ratings.

The transfer of knowledge or skill is a process that is of primary importance in educational projects due to the interest in helping students generalise their learning to settings beyond the initial learning context. Without transfer, most educational or training sessions would be deemed a failure. The ability to transfer learned knowledge or strategies to a novel experience has been linked to the ability for the learner to access the appropriate underlying schema, which may be promoted by the recognition of a pattern in the novel situation that matches prior experience.

The ease of transfer of both knowledge and skill depends heavily upon the perceived similarity of the two tasks. Direct measures of transfer involve providing the learner with a novel problem or situation that resembles the original learning activity in underlying structure, but differs in format, content, or style of presentation. It is valuable to add a measure of transfer of skill or knowledge when measuring achievement, problem solving skills, or critical thinking to demonstrate the breadth of learning obtained in the project.

The measurement of knowledge transfer is most reasonable with direct approximation approaches, either through observation of behaviour in realistic or contrived performance tasks. Indirect measures may include asking teachers to provide estimates of a learner's ability to transfer knowledge or skill to another task or domain. When this method is employed, it is desirable to solicit knowledge transfer estimates in specific conditions or tasks rather than attempting to gather general ratings of learners' knowledge transfer abilities.

Careful construction of assessment tools can often lead to a single measure providing adequate evidence for multiple cognitive dimensions, ranging from academic achievement to creativity. The primary concern when measuring learners' outcomes in the cognitive domain is the degree of fit between the psychological construct and the measurement tool. The use of the terms "direct" and "indirect approximation" underscored the state of affairs regarding cognitive measurement. No scale or performance tool is able to entirely eliminate the problems produced by the learning-performance distinction.

Evaluators need to employ strategies that limit the threats to validity facing programme evaluations that are brought about through the use of tailored tests or measures developed for the unique purpose of evaluating a particular project. First, measures should have adequate reliability and validity prior to making conclusions. In addition to using established measures, reliability and validity can be typically increased by increasing the number of items for each construct. A second effort by evaluators is to gather data on a sufficiently large sample of the target population. Another simple strategy that can be employed to preserve the validity of the data collection process in assessing learner cognition is establishing clear language in all measures.

Regarding development, clarity and structure of language is essential to be sure that young children comprehend the intention of the measurement tool. To assure that young children are comprehending the questions, assessment tools can employ concrete examples or manipulatives, or make use of dynamic assessment practices. Another dimension of clarity involves structuring items and measures in the simplest fashion possible for the target audience to limit the number of misinterpretations participants are likely to make. Finally, the strength of a solid evaluation plan and research design cannot be understated when attempting to provide compelling evidence of cognitive gains.

## Assessment of Affective Measures

Affective measures typically serve two primary purposes in programme evaluation. First, through descriptive analyses, conclusions regarding the impact of the project on the emotional and motivational state of the participants can be formulated. This common use of affective measures provides quality information about projects and is a promising approach for demonstrating a meaningful effect on the learner. The second function of affective measures is far less common, but can also provide compelling and essential data regarding programme efficacy. This involves incorporating the affective construct in causal models or path analyses, examining the power of the affective constructs as mediators.

Exploring student affect such as motivation or interest helps the evaluator identify characteristics of learners for whom the project activities were particularly effective or ineffective. Second, the explanatory power of the model is strengthened due to the inclusion of a personality variable that will influence the replication of results in other settings.

Several evaluation designs involve the use of formative assessments of attitude regarding the state of affairs in the educational setting under review. This formative analysis can be conducted prior to program design in an effort to direct the selection of programme goals, or after an initial period of programme implementation to assess the strengths and weaknesses of plans and products. These formative attitudinal analyses allow the project to be organic and make adjustments based on the initial reactions of the stakeholders. The validity of these formative attitudinal analyses needs to be examined closely due to the unique conditions that are generally present when formative data are collected.

The impact of self-perceptions of ability and skill has been a popular research area since the mid-1970's. The literature on self-efficacy, self-concept, and self-esteem provides evidence regarding the relationships of these constructs with other affective domains, as well as learning and achievement. Self-concept ratings have been found to correlate well with academic achievement, provided the self-concept ratings are not too general in scope.

Self-concept research is almost always based on correlational analyses, the literature has been fixated on establishing the directionality of the relationship between academic self-concept and academic achievement. The notion that self-concept maintains a causal influence over performance is popular and intuitively interesting. This relationship is generally explained through the processes of learned helplessness, motivation or persistence, or self-confidence that allow the individual to perform effectively in evaluative situations. Unfortunately, it is just as plausible to conclude that a sustained pattern of performance determines the individual's self-perception of ability.

Self-esteem is typically identified as an individual's perception of her overall ability, or her ability in a particular domain of skills, along with an evaluative component encompassing how she feels about that ability level. The popularity of self-esteem as a construct is undeniable, and is often identified by policy makers and educational stakeholders as a primary concern in education. Interest in self-esteem likely arise due to the widespread acknowledgement of relationships with academic performance, depression, suicide, social ability, and locus of control.

For this reason, the inclusion of learner self-esteem in evaluation designs is a common practice. However, the evaluation of self-esteem or self-concept should be limited to projects that have an explicit interest in advancing children's self-perceptions, or projects that clearly identify a process through which enhanced self-esteem is expected to facilitate learner success. Although there is a body of research indicating that self-esteem is related to achievement, identifying gains in this dimension should not be treated as evidence that participants have significant gains in learning or achievement.

Self-efficacy is typically conceptualised as a more specific rating of ability than self-esteem or self-concept, and is likened to confidence or comfort with a given activity. Ratings of self-efficacy are of interest to educational researchers and evaluators, especially in the field of educational technology due to the high variability in learner skill. Research has consistently identified strong relationships between self-efficacy and (a) persistence, (b) intrinsic motivation, (c) self-regulated learning, (d) academic achievement, and (e) skill with various technological tools.

As with self-esteem and self-concept, there is a wealth of research pointing to a persistent relationship between self-efficacy and performance. However, it is important to once again clarify that the vast majority of research on self-efficacy and achievement is based on correlational data, limiting the ability to make determinations of a causal relationship between the two constructs.

The process of assessing attitudinal constructs such as motivation, interest, and feelings of comfort differs somewhat from approaches used to evaluate standard cognitive constructs. In particular, the abstract nature of attitudes (and all affective constructs) often leads to a strong reliance on inference. Evaluators often need to rely on inference because (a) attitudes do not lend themselves to direct objective measurement; (b) self-reported attitudes may not be truthful; (c) learners' attitudes, beliefs, and behaviours do not always align; and (d) attitudes are often measured in a single instance, although they are not constant, universal, or stable traits.

The varied approaches to evaluating attitudes can be divided into four core categories: self-report, significant others' reports, sociometric ratings, and behavioural observations. Each methodological approach has both advantages and disadvantages, therefore evaluators should maximise the validity of their data through triangulation, by employing as wide a variety of these strategies as possible.

**Integration of Technology**

Unlike previous technologies, emerging computer-based technology, because of its interactivity, speed, access to multiple sources of inforniation, and potential for cost effectiveness, offers numerous opportunities to achieve the goals proposed by school reformers. The joint implementation of school reform practices and emerging technology should enable educators to:

i) Customise and improve teaching;
ii) Individualise and improve learning;
iii) Achieve equity; and
iv) Effect systemic changes.

Technology is rapidly becoming a dominant force in US schools. Technology is regarded by many as a key element of education reform. Although there is a growing body of research suggesting that technology can enhance and improve learning, there is no consensus as to how this can be accomplished. It is generally recognised, however, that technology by itself is not sufficient to achieve the types of changes envisioned by reformers.

Learning technologies are effective only when treated as one component in implementation strategies that also encompass:

i) curricular reform,
ii) sophisticated and multiple assessments,
iii) effective professional development,
iv) well-maintained technology infrastructures and support systems,
v) attention to equity, and
vi) the restructuring of organisational practices, budgets, and policies.

An exemplary technology-based programme will incorporate all of these dimensions. A promising one may incorporate some of them and will include plans to achieve the remainder. The ultimate goal of the linked elements of any technology programme is increased student learning. Although some may not agree that all of the above elements are necessary to improve learning, the effectiveness of technology will clearly vary with situational variables, such as the goals and resources for instruction, the cognitive demands on the learner, the extent to which all learners' needs are considered, the teachers' comfort and skill with technology, and, of course, the types of technology available.

Thus, "integrated technology" is technology that supports and enhances the achievement of specific teaching and learning goals. For example, if these goals include the mastery of basic arithmetic skills or the development of effective critical thinking skills, the criteria to assess the integration of the technology tools used should include the extent to which these tools contribute to the attainment of these goals in more effective and efficient ways than if more traditional means were utilised.

The Cognition and Technology Group at Vanderbilt [CTGV] has developed a framework for understanding technology and education research. With respect to the educational context, the CTGV model makes a distinction between individual classes and schools, and connected (or networked) classes, schools, and communities. Both the distinction between transmission and constructivist models and the distinction between individual and networked classes or schools have direct implications for technology integration.

Student-centred models are better aligned with the goals of school reform and more likely to put powerful technology tools in the hands of learners. This is particularly important when learning objectives involve higher-order thinking skills, such as the presentation of inforniation in new forms, problemsolving, the analysis of data, the visual representation of ideas, or the analysis and evaluation of a text. Student-centred models also appear to be more appropriate when assessment includes performance-based assessments and the involvement of learners in the identification of the criteria of successful performance.

With respect to networks, the degree of interactivity and access to multiple sources of information are likely to increase with the size of the network. The logic model assumes that the process of technology integration as an educational innovation occurs over time and only if the inputs included in the model are present. In that respect the model is prescriptive. Although only four main inputs have been identified, depending on the characteristics of specific projects other inputs might be included. The first input is access to appropriate technology (for learners and teachers). The second input is technology knowledge and skills so that learners and teachers are comfortable with a variety of technology tools for learning and teaching. The third input is professional development on appropriate models for the integration of technology into the learning environment that teachers can use in the classroom. The fourth input corresponds to the support and structural changes required to effectively integrate technology in schools.

Competent teachers are considered to be a critical intermediate goal—and not a terminal goal—because their improved teaching ability and facility with information technology are means for achieving specific student goals and not ends in themselves. The same can be said of engaged students, the other critical intermediate goal. Student engagement is a necessary but not a sufficient condition for improved academic achievement and improved ability to use technology.

The logic model assumes that technology integration is a process that happens over time and requires certain conditions, referred to as inputs in the model, to take root in the classroom. At the core of the construct of technology integration are the two key intermediate outcomes: competent teachers and engaged students. The measurement of technology integration can be approached in two steps. The first step involves measuring directly the two key intermediate outcomes. This would result in information relative to teachers' actual competency in technology integration, and students' experiences with technology integration. A second step involves measuring the conditions leading to technology integration.

There are two main criteria with respect to technology access are:

i) the availability of technology at school and/or in the classroom, and
ii) access for all students to technology resources.

## RESEARCH ON REFLECTIVE TEACHING

Reflection and reflective teaching are related approaches that have been very fashionable in teacher education and adult education. These approaches are 'intended to prepare teachers to become more thoughtful'. Teaching, however, by definition involves more than just the acquisition of theory about teaching. Implicit or explicit in all the writings that focus upon reflective teaching, other than the extreme position of theorists concerned solely with the personal development of the individual, is that increased reflection will translate into action and result in improvements in teaching and learning.

The range of ideal types of teachers incorporating reflective or inquiry orientated qualities include proposals for the development of self-monitoring teachers, reflective teachers, teachers as continuous experimenters, adaptive teachers, teachers as action researchers, teachers as applied scientists, teachers as moral craftsmen, teachers as problem solvers, teachers as hypothesis makers, teachers as clinical inquirers, self-analytic teachers, teachers as radical pedagogues, teachers as political craftsmen and scholar teachers. Clearly, there is competition between these various positions and ideals, which can only be resolved through close comparison and evaluation of practical outcomes from teacher education programmes based on recommended strategies and stated objectives for each philosophical position.

What is desirable is not simply a testing of paradigms in opposition to reflective approaches, but a testing of conflicting reflective paradigms to determine the most relevant and effective for educational practice. Unless this occurs teacher education programmes, which utilise reflective approaches in the most effective ways, are unlikely to be developed. More generally, the credibility of reflective teaching and its continued usage with beginning teachers are dependent upon demonstration of significant long-term benefits. The continued useful existence of any paradigm or model is dependent upon that approach being demonstrably superior in some way to existing or competing paradigms, or better able to explain observable phenomena. If a paradigm is unable to demonstrate this, then it will either be ignored by knowledgeable practitioners, or the useful, proven sections incorporated into other theory or paradigms which can better explain observed phenomena and/or are more useful in practice.

The history of teacher education reveals only too clearly that, in the longer term, paradigms or approaches that fail to prove effective or superior fall out of favour, for example, micro-teaching, and are replaced by other approaches. Comparing teachers who had graduated recently, and some time before from conventional colleges and colleges implementing reflective teaching programmes, found no differences between the two groups in attitude to reflection and inclination towards innovation.

Reflection and generalisation of self-analyses to others are also important components in much European philosophy, and reflection is likely to be perceived sympathetically for that reason. The writings of Aristotle, Plato and Socrates, founders of educational thinking, abound with accounts of self-analytical thinking. However, separation of the theoretical and practical as is encouraged by many reflective approaches is not at all productive.

Technical teaching skills and techniques are essential for effective classroom management and learning by students. Furthermore, they are of great concern to beginning teachers. It is worth noting that those recruiting teachers still place possession of. technical teaching skills high on the list of necessary abilities and qualifications. Other, also essential, foundational knowledge for effective teaching are the three areas identified.

These are subject content knowledge, pedagogical knowledge, that is knowledge about teaching and learning, and pedagogical content knowledge, that is knowledge derived from teaching experience of the more difficult area for students and how to teach these areas more effectively. No less essential are knowledge of social issues, history of educational movements and professional attitudes and practices. In tackling the important issues of what is involved in effective learning, how a teacher should select, structure and present material, and consideration of the forces shaping society and education, there is ample opportunity for teacher educators to establish a firm foundation for the development of critical thinking which is essential to drive effective teaching performance.

However, the developmental needs of teachers to develop teaching survival skills needs to be the priority in early stages and not be swamped by social idealism. Firm focus upon the realities of learning and about truly effective teaching may have the additional benefit of providing a firmer focus and structure for teacher education courses generally. There is one consistent message that emerges from consideration of the enthusiasm for reflective teaching paradigms. This is that all new paradigms should be assessed in an empirical way before there is wide scale adoption.

Educational decision makers realised that wide-scale implementation of new approaches, which satisfy short-term social or political imperatives before empirical assessment via thorough, smaller scale trials, may be counter-productive in the longer term. Simply rushing to join in a fashion in an uncritical way seems the height of social irresponsibility and a denial of possession of truly critical skills of analysis, which it would be expected that teacher educators and policy makers should possess.

The generic nature of reflective teaching approaches are 'intended to prepare teachers to become more thoughtful'. Teaching, however, by definition involves more than just the acquisition of theory about teaching. Implicit or explicit in all the writings that focus upon reflective teaching, other than the extreme position of theorists concerned solely with the personal development of the individual, is that increased reflection will translate into action and result in improvements in teaching and learning.

Despite a common generic base and ideals of action to bring about educational change, the terminology used by different writers reflects different epistemological positions and traditions that result in the expression of often radically different theoretical ideals. Tom (1985, p. 36) has drawn attention to the range of ideal types of teachers incorporating reflective or inquiry orientated qualities. These include proposals for the development of self-monitoring teachers, reflective teachers, teachers as continuous experimenters, adaptive teachers, teachers as action researchers, teachers as applied scientists, teachers as moral craftsmen, teachers as problem solvers, teachers as hypothesis makers, teachers as clinical inquirers, self-analytic teachers, teachers as radical pedagogues, teachers as political craftsmen and scholar teachers.

Clearly, there is competition between these various positions and ideals, which can only be resolved through close comparison and evaluation of practical outcomes from teacher education programmes based on recommended strategies and stated objectives for each philosophical position. In fact, one would have anticipated that there would have been concerted efforts to evaluate the practical effectiveness of these various approaches by empirical methods and through that the ideological positions that they represent, but this has not occurred to any appreciable degree.

Furthermore, without adequate definition, there is little chance of agreement upon objectives or desired outcomes as teacher educators strive to select course and subject content, and utilise processes to achieve the ideals. More generally, the credibility of reflective teaching and its continued usage with beginning teachers are dependent upon demonstration of significant long-term benefits. The continued useful existence of any paradigm or model is dependent upon that approach being demonstrably superior in some way to existing or competing paradigms, or better able to explain observable phenomena.

If a paradigm is unable to demonstrate this, then it will either be ignored by knowledgeable practitioners, or the useful, proven sections incorporated into other theory or paradigms which can better explain observed phenomena and/or are more useful in practice.

The few significant differences found indicated that those entering reflective programmes with higher level reflective skills were able to reflect better, that subjects experiencing reflective teaching were better able to think and talk about teaching, and reported feeling less anxiety about practice teaching. Counter-balancing these findings are non-significant results from comparison of experimental and control groups for student teaching grades, and identifying more variables present in the act of teaching. Furthermore, reflective treatment groups did not reveal a more realistic view of the role and demands of teaching.

There appear to be two sets of issues that are deserving of analysis in the light of the failure to demonstrate empirically any superiority of reflective teaching approaches. There is an almost infinitesimal number of possible variations of reflective ideals possible when differences in individuals' ability to acquire and process information, specialisation or occupation, and cultural, religious, political, social class and gender variables are taken into account. Reflection needs to be predicated upon both something to think about and the ability to engage in critical thinking. That is, there must be content or a coherent body of knowledge and logical processing skills.

Systematic reflective thinking about teaching is predicated upon a broad and indepth understanding of what is happening in the classroom. This implies that there is a need for quite sophisticated understanding of teaching and related activities before it is possible to engage in effective reflective teaching practices. Selection of content, and provision of teaching experiences likely to foster understanding of the links between teaching and learning, thus remain as important issues in teacher education courses. The types of processes that have often been selected and implemented in reflective teacher education may also have been selected on the basis of incorrect assumptions.

While there are numerous accounts of strategies and techniques which can be employed to assist trainee teachers develop reflective capacity, there do not appear to be any accounts of helping to develop logical thinking skills. Many accounts of reflection in adult learning theory or reflective teaching assume that students already possess the skills and knowledge necessary for effective, critical thinking. In very few cases does there appear to be any recognition that these skills need to be taught and developed quite explicitly.

**Developmental Continuum of Teacher Learning**

There is ample evidence in all learning that those with a richer knowledge base get richer and this, in itself, suggests a developmental continuum. Despite this, the developmental aspects of teaching skill acquisition, which have been identified by a number of researchers, appear to have been almost totally ignored in the reflective literature. This is something of an inconsistency, since beginning teachers are those most focused upon and considered most likely to benefit from reflective teacher education experiences.

Another serious weakness inherent in many reflective paradigms is the failure to take account of a long recognised problem in human learning—forgetting. Simply being critical is not enough either to guarantee that those critical thoughts will be remembered or that those thoughts can be translated into effective procedural action. For example, can the reader clearly recall all the issues that were reflected upon on Monday last week? While keeping of diaries and other records is one avenue to addressing this problem, and those advocating action learning and reflection via micro-teaching address some issues of connecting learning to doing to facilitate retention, none of the approaches takes heed of the need for substantial practice and feedback over extended periods of time to develop skills.

The time frames of most programmes attempting to develop sophisticated performance and thinking skills for complex natural classrooms, and change deeply ingrained values and attitudes of novice teachers, are frankly totally unrealistic. Furthermore, most experienced teacher educators would consider that values and attitudes are more difficult to change than to develop specific performance skills.

In the 1980s and early 1990s the initial effects of the technological and economic revolutions were starting to be felt. Demands for more effective schooling and post-compulsory education emerged as the competition from developing Asian nations came to be felt, with these demands being reflected in all kinds of government reports. The need to think more creatively and effectively to become more competitive and improve work productivity seems an obvious solution. It is probable that the adoption of reflective practices also had much to do with the reduction of funding to teacher education during this period of economic rationalism. It seems almost as if teacher educators really believed that they could achieve more with less through establishing a teacher education objective of better thinking for novice teachers.

## IMPLICATIONS OF TEACHER SELF-EFFICACY

Social cognitive theory assumes that people are capable of human agency, or intentional pursuit of courses of action, and that such agency operates in a process called triadic reciprocal causation. Self-efficacy is beliefs in one's capabilities to organise and execute the courses of action required to produce given attainments. This beliefs were characterised as the major mediators for our behavior, and importantly, behavioral change. Educationally, self-efficacy beliefs are related to academic performance and self-regulated learning. This efficacy beliefs help dictate motivation.

From the social cognitive theory perspective, because human agency is mediated by our efficaciousness, self-efficacy beliefs influence our choices, our effort, our persistence when facing adversity, and our emotions. Unfortunately, teacher efficacy research has at times been theoretically confused. Consistent with the general formulation of self-efficacy, Tschannen-Moran and Woolfolk Hoy defined teacher efficacy as a teacher's "judgment of his or her capabilities to bring about desired outcomes of student engagement and learning, even among those students who may be difficult or unmotivated."

Unfortunately, researchers' interpretations of these theories have significantly muddied the efficacy waters as regards the theoretical formulation of teacher efficacy and the psychometric attempts to measure the construct. The correlates of teacher efficacy are many when using a variety of efficacy scales and measurements. Students of efficacious teachers generally have outperformed students in other classes. Teacher efficacy is also related to students' own sense of efficacy and student motivation.

Regarding teacher behaviours, efficacious teachers persist with struggling students and criticise less after incorrect student answers. Teachers with high efficacy tend to experiment with methods of instruction, seek improved teaching methods, and experiment with instructional materials. The study of teacher efficacy has borne much fruit. Accordingly, teacher efficacy is presently on the precipice of inquiry; it is ready to either move forward or fall to the wayside as a good idea that ultimately had little substance.

Social cognitive theory provides the theoretical foundation for teacher efficacy. There are four sources of efficacy building information:

i) mastery experiences,
ii) vicarious experiences,
iii) social persuasion, and
iv) physiological or emotional arousal.

Mastery experiences are considered the most powerful influence on efficacy as they provide direct feedback regarding capabilities. However, because the feedback "must be processed and weighed through self-referent thought," all success does not lead to bolstered efficacy. Attributional analysis and causal assumptions concerning outcomes impact the interpretation of mastery experiences. Furthermore, some outcomes may be valued more than others. For example, a teacher may succeed at altering an assignment to the appropriate level of a student, but experience no increase in confidence because no special value was vested in the outcome.

Social cognitive theory emphasises that vicarious experiences can impact learning and efficacy. Social persuasion and the emotional state that one experiences during social interactions can also bolster, or weaken, self-efficacy beliefs. If teacher efficacy is the powerful predictive construct it has been thought to be, then research examining the processes by which such efficacy is built is critical to fostering teacher efficacy and, ultimately, changing behavior.

Recently some researchers have begun to explore the construct of collective teacher efficacy. Because social cognitive theory holds that "personal agency operates within a broad network of sociostructural influences" the theory "extends the analysis of mechanisms of human agency to the exercise of collective agency". Collective efficacy takes self-efficacy to the social level. Teacher efficacy research must grapple with the issue of efficacy change.

Current evidence suggests that teacher efficacy is indeed malleable, but that change will likely occur only via engaging and meaningful professional development opportunities, particularly activities such as teacher research initiatives that capitalise on teachers' critical thought and human agency.

## References

Allinder, R. M., "The relationships between efficacy and the instructional practices of special education teachers and consultants", *Teacher Education and Special Education*, 17, 86-95, 1994.

Anderson, R, Greene, M., & Loewen, P., "Relationships among teachers' and students' thinking skills, sense of efficacy, and student achievement", *Alberta Journal of Educational Research*, 34(2), 148-165, 1988.

Bassey, M, and Constable, H., "Higher education research in education 1992 to 1996: fields of enquiry reported in the RAE", *Research Intelligence*, 61, BERA, July, 1977.

Bandura, A., *Social foundations of thought and action: A social cognitive theory*, Englewood Cliffs, NJ: Prentice-Hall, 1986.

Boyer, E.L., Teaching's renewed role in evaluation of learning, *Times Higher Education Supplement*, 1990

Brown, G and Atkins, M., *Effective Teaching in Higher Education,* Methuen, London, 1988.

_______________ , Bull, J., and Pendlebury, M., *Assessing Student Learning in Higher Education,* Routledge, London, 1997.

Chickering, A. W., and Gamson, Z. F., "Seven Principles of Good Practice in Undergraduate Education", *AAHE Bulletin*, 39, 3-7, 1987.

Cochran-Smith, M, and Lytle, S., "Research on teaching and teacher research: The issues that divide", *Educational Researcher*, 19, 2-11, 1990.

Coladarci, T., "Teachers' sense of efficacy and commitment to teaching", *Journal of Experimental Education*, 60, 323-337, 1992.

Elton, L and Partington, P., *Teaching Standards and Excellence in Higher Education Developing a Culture for Quality*, 2nd edn, CVCP/USD, Sheffield, 1993.

Guskey, T. R., "Teacher efficacy, self-concept, and attitudes toward the implementation of instructional innovation", *Teaching and Teacher Education*, 4, 63-69, 1988.

Hounsell, D., "Documenting and assessing excellent teachers, in Evaluating Teacher Quality in Higher Education", ed. R. Aylett and K. Gregory, Falmer, London, 1996.

Pajares, F., "Current directions in self-efficacy research", In M. Maehr & P. R. Pintrich (Eds.), *Advances in motivation and achievement* (Vol. 10, pp. 1-49), Greenwich, CT: JAI Press, 1997.

Shneiderman, B., *Designing the user interface: Strategies for effective human-computer-interaction*, Addison Wesley Longman, 1998.

Shulman, L., "Knowledge and teaching: Foundations of the new reform", *Harvard Educational Review*, 57(1), 1-22, 1987.

# 9

# Effective Teaching in Varied Subjects

The scope and value attached to any teaching/research linkages will depend fundamentally on how each activity itself is conceptualised. For example, the simple dichotomous view recently expressed in Coaldrake and Stedman that research is 'the generation of new knowledge' and teaching is the 'transmission of knowledge', then many academics who want to integrate them can be seen as wishfully pursuing a 'romantic preference'. Yet such clear binary definitions are seldom adequate to the real complexity of either teaching or research in practice. 'Transmission' implies teacher-dominated instruction and ignores the substantial move towards more self-directed and distributed forms of learning. And this move has come about partly because educational research shows that people learn best when they have some control over certain elements in the process of acquiring knowledge.

The relationship between teaching and research can never be satisfactorily demonstrated. Learning however is the vital link between research and teaching. It is a shared process in these two enterprises. Learning acts as a powerful intervening factor in all of the studies attempting to demonstrate a relationship between teaching and research since it is the process whereby an individual—teacher, researcher, student, learner—comes to know.

Research is wholly about learning, any more than facilitating learning is the whole of teaching. But it is the significant and substantial element that they share.

Teaching and research are correlated when they are correlated, i.e., when what is being related are two aspects of the same activity: learning.

During the early years of school, the exploration of the concepts of likenesses and differences in school subjects such as language arts, mathematics, science, music, and art makes the study of culture appropriate. Socially, the young learner is beginning to interact with other students, some of whom are like the student and some different; naturally, he or she wants to know more about others. In the middle grades, students begin to explore and ask questions about the nature of culture and specific aspects of culture, such as language and beliefs, and the influence of those aspects on human behaviour.

As students progress through high school, they can understand and use complex cultural concepts such as adaptation, assimilation, acculturation, diffusion, and dissonance drawn from anthropology, sociology, and other disciplines to explain how culture and cultural systems function. Cultural diversity is a fact of existence in every modern-day society and few nations or empires in the past were void of such diversity. The challenge of all people is, wherever and whenever possible, to consider the strengths and advantages that this diversity offers to the society in.general, and to their own growth as a human being in particular.

Teachers of social studies at all school levels should provide developmentally appropriate experiences as they guide learners in the study of culture and cultural diversity. They should:

i) enable learners to analyse and explain the ways groups, societies, and cultures address human needs and concerns;
ii) guide learners as they predict how data and experiences may be interpreted by people from diverse cultural perspectives and frames of reference;
iii) assist learners to apply an understanding of culture as an integrated whole that explains the functions and

interactions of language, literature, the arts, traditions, beliefs and values, and behavior patterns;

iv) encourage learners to compare and analyse societal patterns for preserving and transmitting culture while adapting to environmental or social change;

v) enable learners to give examples and describe the importance of cultural unity and diversity within and across groups;

vi) have learners interpret patterns of behavior reflecting values and attitudes that contribute or pose obstacles to cross-cultural understanding;

vii) guide learners as they construct reasoned judgments about specific cultural responses to persistent human issues;

viii) have learners explain and apply ideas, theories, and modes of inquiry drawn from anthropology and sociology in the examination of persistent issues and social problems.

Teachers at various school levels should build upon learners' knowledge, experience, and developmental capabilities. Teachers of the early grades can assist learners to explore, comprehend, and apply critical information, ideas, and concepts that are common across societies, social institutions, cultures, and cultural perspectives. They can help learners comprehend cultural universals, such as norms, folkways, sanctions, social institutions, arts, and taboos and then use them to analyse their own and other cultures. They can use comparisons of cultures or subcultures and their perspectives, whether they exist in the present or past, to highlight contextual understanding.

Socially, the young learner can be actively and frequently interacting in appropriate ways with other students, some of whom are like the learner and some different. These interactions can be encouraged and monitored and can involve rather than avoid dialogues about the substance of one's culture and perspectives. Teachers of the middle grades can assist learners to explore and ask questions about the nature of culture that provide a wider range of cultural universals and indepth study of the specific aspects of particular cultures in similar and different places, times, conditions, and contexts.

Teachers can encourage learners to consider the direct and indirect connections between the assumptions, beliefs, and values of a culture and its actions, policies, and products in multiple situations. They can help them analyse the ways that a people's cultural ideas and actions influence its members. Through this inquiry, learners can begin to consider such phenomenon as cultural lag, assimilation, accommodation, and the strength of the impact traditions have on thought and action within any particular social group.

High school teachers can assist learners deepen their comprehension and increase their application of cultural concepts already studied, such as cultural lag, assimilation, accommodation, and the impact of traditions on thought and action within any particular social group. They can also introduce new concepts such as the function and interactions of language, literature, and the arts in terms of traditions, beliefs, and values; and the transmitting of culture in the face of environmental, technical, and social change.

Learners should be able to engage independently in indepth analysis of any cultural group or subgroup and indepth comparison of any two or more cultural groups or subgroups. They should be able to connect their comprehension of cultural groups to the realities of cultural diversity within multicultural societies and consider how culturally different groups can cooperate to enhance the public good.

In the middle grades, students, through a more formal study of history, continue to expand their understanding of the past and of historical concepts and inquiry. They begin to understand and appreciate differences in historical perspectives, recognising that interpretations are influenced by individual experiences, societal values, and cultural traditions. High school students engage in more sophisticated analysis and reconstruction of the past, examining its relationship to the present and extrapolating into the future. They integrate individual stories about people, events, and situations to form a more holistic.conception, in which continuity and change are linked in time and across cultures. Students also learn to draw on their knowledge of history to make informed choices and decisions in the present.

Teachers of social studies at all school levels should provide developmentally appropriate experiences as they guide learners in the study of time, continuity and change. They should:

i) assist learners to understand that historical knowledge and the concept of time are socially influenced constructions that lead historians to be selective in the questions they seek to answer and the evidence they use;
ii) help learners apply key concepts such as time, chronology, causality, change, conflict, and complexity to explain, analyse, and show connections among patterns of historical change and continuity;
iii) enable learners to identify and describe significant historical periods and patterns of change within and across cultures, such as the development of ancient cultures and civilisations, the rise of nation states, and social, economic, and political revolutions;
iv) guide learners as they systematically employ processes of critical historical inquiry to reconstruct and interpret the past, such as using a variety of sources and checking their credibility, validating and weighing evidence for claims, and searching for causality;
v) provide learners with opportunities to investigate, interpret, and analyse multiple historical and contemporary viewpoints within and across cultures related to important events, recurring dilemmas, and persistent issues, while employing empathy, skepticism, and critical judgement;
v) enable learners to apply ideas, theories, and modes of historical inquiry to analyse historical and

contemporary developments, and to inform and evaluate actions concerning public policy issues.

Middle grade teachers can facilitate the understanding and appreciation of differences in historical perspectives, and the recognition that interpretations are influenced by individual experiences, societal values, and cultural traditions. High school teachers can engage learners in a sophisticated analysis and reconstruction of the past, helping them to examine the relationship of the past to the present and extrapolating into the future. Teachers can facilitate learners' integration of individual stories about people, events, and.situations so that they might form a holistic conception, in which continuity and change are linked in time and across cultures.

Teachers can help learners to draw on their knowledge of history to make informed choices and decisions in the present. Technological advances connect students at all levels to the world beyond their personal locations. The study of people, places, and human-environment interactions assists learners as they create their spatial views and geographic perspectives of the world.

Personal identity is shaped by one's culture, by groups, and by institutional influences. While much of what humans are and become has been associated with genetics and assumed natural stages of physical, psychological, emotional, and mental development, a far greater factor in personal and identity construction and application is the interaction of the individual with his or her environments and the consequences of these interactions. All individuals should know the factors that contribute to who they are; to what they think, feel, and believe; and to why they are likely to make certain decisions and act in particular ways. Furthermore, they need to understand the relationship between social norms and emerging personal identities, the social processes that influence identity formation, and the ethical principles underlying individual action.

Institutions such as schools, churches, families, government agencies, and the courts play an integral role in people's lives. These and other institutions exert enormous influence over us, yet institutions are no more than organisational embodiments to further the core social values of those who comprise them. Thus, it is important that students learn how institutions are formed, what controls and influences them, how they influence individuals and culture, and how they are maintained or changed.

Young children should be given opportunities to examine various institutions that affect their lives and influence their thinking. They should be assisted in recognising the tensions that occur when the goals, values, and principles of two or more institutions or groups conflict—for example, when the school board prohibits candy machines in schools vs. a class project to install a candy machine to help raise money for the local hospital. They should also have opportunities to explore ways in which institutions such as churches or health care networks are created to respond to changing individual and group needs. Middle school learners will benefit from varied experiences through which they examine the ways in which institutions change over time, promote social conformity, and influence culture. They should be encouraged to use this understanding to suggest ways to work through institutional change for the common good. High school students must understand the paradigms and traditions that undergird social and political institutions. They should be provided opportunities to examine, use, and add to the body of knowledge related to the behavioural sciences and social theory as it relates to the ways people and groups organise themselves around common needs, beliefs, and interests.

By examining the purposes and characteristics of various governance systems, learners develop an understanding of how groups and nations attempt to resolve conflicts and seek to establish order and security. Through study of the dynamic relationships among individual rights and responsibilities, the needs of social groups, and concepts of a just society, learners become more effective problem-solvers and decision-makers when addressing the persistent issues and social problems encountered in public life. They do so by applying concepts and methods of political science and law.

In schools, this theme typically appears in units and courses dealing with government, politics, political science, history, law, and other social sciences. Learners in the early grades explore their natural and developing sense of fairness and order as they experience relationships with others. They develop an increasingly comprehensive awareness of rights and responsibilities in specific contexts. During the middle school years, these rights and responsibilities are applied in more complex contexts with emphasis on new applications.

Teachers of social studies at all school levels should provide developmentally appropriate experiences as they guide learners in the study of power, authority, and governance. They should:

i) enable learners to examine the rights and responsibilities of the individual in relation to his or her family, social groups, community, and nation;

ii) help students to understand the purpose of government and how its powers are acquired, used, and justified;

iii) provide opportunities for learners to examine issues involving the rights, roles, and status of individuals in relation to the general welfare;

iv) enable learners to describe the ways nations and organisations respond to forces of unity and diversity affecting order and security;

v) have learners explain conditions, actions, and motivations that contribute to conflict and cooperation within and among nations;

vi) help learners to analyse and explain governmental mechanisms to meet the needs and wants of citizens, regulate territory, manage conflict, and establish order and security;

vii) have learners identify and describe the basic features of the American political system, and identify representative leaders from various levels and branches of government;

viii) challenge learners to apply concepts such as power, role, status, justice, and influence to the examination of persistent issues and social problems;

xi) guide learners to explain how governments attempt to achieve their stated ideals at home and abroad.

Teachers of the early grades can assist learners in exploring their natural and developing sense of fairness and order as they experience relationships with others. Learners should develop an increasingly comprehensive awareness of rights and responsibilities. For example, learners can examine the rules, types of authority, and governmental structures of their schools and communities. Teachers of the middle grades can help learners apply these rights and responsibilities in specific contexts. During these years, learners can apply these rights and responsibilities in increasing complex situations with emphasis upon new applications.

High school teachers can help learners develop their abilities in the use of abstract principles. At this level, learners can study various systems that have been developed over the centuries to allocate and employ power and authority in the governance process. For example, they can compare structures and authority roles in monarchies, dictatorships, oligarchies, and democracies. They can also study local and national power situations and respond to them intellectually and in action as developing citizens who are reaching the age to vote.

Young learners begin by differentiating between wants and needs. They explore economic decisions as they compare their own economic experiences with those of others and consider the wider consequences of those decisions on groups, communities, the nation, and beyond. In the middle grades, learners expand their knowledge of economic concepts and principles, and use economic reasoning processes in addressing issues related to the four fundamental economic questions. High school students develop economic perspectives and deeper understanding of key economic concepts and processes through systematic study of a range of economic and sociopolitical systems, with particular emphasis on the examination of domestic and global economic policy options related to matters such as health care, resource use, unemployment, and trade.

Science is an enterprise that focuses on inquiry about natural phenomena; technology is the designing of things and processes to achieve practical purposes. Learners need to realise that both science and technology have had a profound effect in shaping human experience and the world around us. Technology is as old as the first crude tool invented by prehistoric humans, but today's technology forms the basis for some of our most difficult social choices.

Young children can learn how technologies form systems and how their daily lives are intertwined with a host of technologies. They can study how basic technologies such as ships, automobiles, and airplanes have evolved and how we have employed technology such as air conditioning, dams, and irrigation to modify our physical environment. From history (their own and others'), they can construct examples of how technologies such as the wheel, the stirrup, and the transistor radio altered the course of history. By the middle grades, students can begin to explore the complex relationships among technology, human values, and behavior.

Teachers of social studies at all school levels should provide developmentally appropriate experiences as they guide learners in the study of science and technology. They should:

i) enable learners to identify, describe, and examine both current and historical examples of the interaction and interdependence of science, technology, and society in a variety of cultural settings;

ii) provide opportunities for learners to make judgments about how science and technology have transformed the physical world and human society and our understanding of time, space, place, and human-environment interactions;

iii) have learners analyse the way in which science and technology influence core societal values, beliefs, and attitudes and how societal attitudes shape scientific and technological change;

iv) prompt learners to evaluate various policies proposed to deal with social changes resulting from new technologies;

v) help learners to identify and interpret various perspectives about human societies and the physical world using scientific knowledge, technologies, and ethical standards from diverse world cultures;

vi) encourage learners to formulate strategies and develop policy proposals for influencing public discussions associated with science/technology-society issues.

Teachers of the early grades can help learners use their own experiences with science and technology to develop an understanding of the role that science and technology play in shaping human experience. They can have them consider how inventions have altered the course of history and how society has employed technologies to modify the physical environment. They can also provide opportunities for learners to consider instances in which changes in values, beliefs, and attitudes have resulted from the communication and acceptance of scientific and technological knowledge.

Teachers of young learners can also challenge them to consider ways to monitor science and technology to protect the physical environment, individual rights, and the common good. Teachers of the middle grades can provide opportunities for learners to extend their understanding of the roles that science and technology play in their own lives and in the lives of others. They can help learners identify examples of how science and technology have transformed individuals' lives and social institutions and how they have changed people's perceptions of and beliefs about the natural and social world.

They can ask learners to weigh the need for laws and policies to govern scientific activities and technological applications. They can also challenge them to seek and consider reasonable and ethical alternatives to issues that arise when scientific theories, discoveries, or findings and social norms or religious beliefs come into conflict. High school teachers can provide opportunities for learners to deepen their understanding of the roles that science and technology have played historically and contemporaneously in transforming the physical world and human society and how we can manage change rather than be controlled by it. They can provide opportunities for learners to confront issues involving science and technology and in so doing, guide learners as they analyse the reciprocal influence.that scientific inquiry and technology and core social values and beliefs have upon one another.

The realities of global interdependence require understanding the increasingly important and diverse global connections among world societies. Emerging global issues in many fields are:

i) health care
ii) economic development
iii) economic interdependence
iv) environmental quality
v) universal human rights
vi) ethnic enmities
vii) political and military alliances

Analysing patterns and relationships within and among world cultures helps learners carefully examine policy alternatives that have both national and global implications. This theme typically appears in units or courses dealing with geography, culture, and economics, but again can draw upon the natural and physical sciences and the humanities, including literature, the arts, and language.

Teachers of social studies at all school levels should provide developmentally appropriate experiences as they guide learners in the study of global connections and interdependence. They should:

i) enable learners to explain how language, art, music, belief systems, and other cultural elements can facilitate global understanding or cause misunderstanding;.
ii) help learners to explain conditions and motivations that contribute to conflict,cooperation, and interdependence among groups, societies, and nations;
iii) provide opportunities for learners to analyse and evaluate the effects of changing technologies on the global community;
iv) challenge learners to analyse the causes, consequences, and possible solutions to persistent, contemporary, and emerging global issues, such as health care, security, resource allocation, economic development, and environmental quality;
v) guide learner analysis of the relationships and tensions between national sovereignty and global interests in such matters as territorial disputes, economic development, nuclear and other weapons deployment, use of natural resources, and human rights concerns;
vi) have learners analyse or formulate policy statements in such ways that they demonstrate an understanding of concerns, standards, issues, and conflicts related to universal human rights;
vii) help learners to describe and evaluate the role of international and multinational organisations in the global arena;
viii) have learners illustrate how individual behaviors and decisions connect with global systems.

Teachers of the middle grades can encourage learners to initiate analyses of the interactions among states and nations and their cultural complexities as they respond to global events and changes. They might encourage learners to explore the causes, consequences, and possible solutions to persistent, contemporary, and emerging global issues or have learners describe and explain various specific instances of tensions between national sovereignty and global interests.

High school teachers can assist learners in thinking systematically about personal, national, and global decisions, interactions, and consequences, including addressing critical issues such as peace, human rights, trade, and global ecology. They might ask learners to formulate policy statements that demonstrate an understanding of concerns, standards, issues, and conflicts related to universal human rights, or to illustrate how individual behaviors and decisions connect with global systems.

Teachers of the early grades can introduce learners to civic ideals and practices through activities such as involving them in the establishment of classroom rules and expectations and determining how to balance the needs of individuals and the group. Teachers of the middle grades can help learners expand their ability to analyse and evaluate the relationships between ideals and practice. In addition, they can provide opportunities for learners to envision taking civic roles in their communities.

High school teachers can help learners recognise the rights and responsibilities of citisens in identifying societal needs, setting directions for public policies, and working to support both individual dignity and the common good. In addition, they can provide opportunities for learners to experience participation in community service and political activities and develop skill in using the democratic process to influence public policy.

## Learning Disabilities in Varied Subjects

Learning disabilities are by far the most common disability among school-age children—more than half of students with disabilities are learning disabled. Generally, students with learning disabilities have difficulties in listening, speaking, reading, writing, reasoning, or mathematics. They also often have trouble sustaining attention to task; remembering procedures, deadlines, and verbal information; and applying organisational skills.

In mathematics and science, students with learning disabilities frequently have difficulty with computation, problem solving, terminology, making inferences, and integrating new and prior knowledge. Memory, motor, and attention deficits are also common and impact students' mathematics and science achievement. Learning difficulties in certain areas, such as in language or organisational skills, they may be gifted in other domains, such as in art or performance. These students' talents or intellectual gifts are often overshadowed by their weaknesses.

Thus, teachers will want to identify and support students' strengths and interests as well as address their disabilities. When a teacher recognises and supports the intellectual and personal strengths of a student with a learning disability, he will likely raise that child's self-confidence and heighten her determination to persevere.

The general education teacher is responsible for ensuring that students with learning disabilities learn the same core content and concepts as all other students in the class. Today's standards reform and inclusion movements mean that expectations for all students have risen sharply. Some educators and parents are wary of aspects of the new standards and inclusion practices, which they see as potentially placing higher expectations on students without providing necessary support.

The principles of inclusion, multiculturalism, and special education can be powerful coagents, creating environments in which each child can flourish. These principles focus on identifying and responding to the individual learning needs of young people; ensuring that all students learn important concepts and skills in the core academic content; and conducting equitable and authentic assessments of students' knowledge.

Teachers must be aware of this issue when considering whether to refer a child for special education. For all students—including those children who are currently in a special education program—teachers need to understand their cultural and language differences as well as their learning differences. When teachers are aware of the roles culture and language play in the learning styles and needs of students, they will likely perceive students' abilities and disabilities more accurately and respond more effectively.

The physical arrangement of the classroom can influence the learning environment. Teachers will want to be sure that students with learning disabilities are seated in ways that do not distance them from the teacher or the primary locus of learning. Though grouping students of similar abilities together can be appropriate to achieve some learning goals, students should frequently be paired or grouped with students of mixed abilities. Also, students with learning disabilities should share in meaningful tasks and take their turn at leadership roles.

The effectiveness of cooperative learning in mathematics and science is well established by research. Cooperative learning can improve students' academic achievement and help them to develop greater self-confidence, more cross-cultural understanding, and enhanced social skills. In mathematics, students often improve their problem-solving abilities and solve more abstract mathematical problems when studying cooperatively.

In science, cooperative learning tends to raise the level of discourse. Students gain skills in clarifying, defending, elaborating, evaluating, and arguing with one another about concepts and scientific methods.

In peer tutoring, a student with a learning disability is paired with a student who does not have a learning disability. Typically, the student without disabilities will function as tutor, helping the tutee with tasks which require additional practice. Teachers will want to ensure that tutors understand their role and responsibilities, and understand the task to be used during tutoring. Teachers should demonstrate effective interpersonal skills, including how to provide corrective feedback.

Learning objectives for the tutoring session should be clearly specified, and a formative assessment component can be put in place to monitor the student's progress. Peer tutoring typically benefits the tutor as well as the taught. Teachers will want to monitor and assess students' progress throughout instruction, not just at the end of a unit. Formative assessments enable diverse learners to show their knowledge in various ways, for example, by writing, demonstrating, modelling, or by representing their ideas orally or graphically. This provides teachers with valuable insight into students' prior knowledge, academic progress, and thinking processes.

Formative assessments also document the effectiveness of the curriculum and instructional strategies. Thus, teachers can use formative assessments to inform their future classroom practices. Performance assessments also provide teachers with insight into students' reasoning and thinking processes. These assessments focus on the process of solving problems or completing complex tasks, emphasising what students can do, not just what they know. Performance assessments allow students to show how they reach their solutions, explain their answers, and demonstrate their ability to synthesize information.

In performance assessment, teachers typically observe students as they work, interview students about their work, and examine products that students have produced. Paper-and-pencil tasks that require students to show their work or describe their procedures will also give teachers insights into students' problem-solving strategies.

Rubrics also can be used to assess the achievement of students with learning disabilities. Rubrics are standards against which a student's work is compared and judged. There are two types of rubrics, analytic and holistic. Holistic rubrics focus on the total performance or final product rather than the individual steps taken to arrive at the final product. Therefore, analytic rubrics may be most appropriate for use with students with learning disabilities because they are more process oriented.

The special education teacher can support the efforts of the general education teacher by briefing him on students' developing histories, students' academic strengths and weaknesses, and education plans that have been most successful. The special education teacher can help brainstorm curriculum ideas or modify an assignment for an individual student. She can provide appropriate materials, teach part of a lesson, and arrange for additional support in the classroom or in a separate location.

Teachers and families need to be united in their efforts to assist children in developing to their fullest. Teachers can foster collaborative relationships with families by being aware of the challenges families face and how these challenges impact parents' involvement in their children's education. For example, some parents of students with learning disabilities share their child's disability and may have had negative experiences in school that make them reluctant to talk to school officials.

Some families have an extended family network whose members may play an important role in the child's development. These individuals may help parents to retain key information from school meetings when parents are feeling overwhelmed and may play a key role in implementing intervention strategies.

Big ideas are important concepts or principles that help students to organise, connect, and apply component facts and ideas. When students learn scientific facts, ideas, and processes as part of an overarching theme, or big idea, they are more likely to see meaningful relationships between science and other disciplines, as well as with their own lives. Interdisciplinary themes can link various science disciplines—such as biology, chemistry, earth science, and physics—or relate science to other subject areas, such as mathematics, English, social studies, and art.

When selecting themes around which to organise instruction, teachers will want to consider several factors: the alignment of curriculum to content standards; the relevance of the themes to students' lives; whether the themes will provide sufficient opportunities to teach fundamental and higher-level content and skills; the length of time it will take to complete the unit; and availability of materials and resources.

The design of theme-based science lessons should not only integrate key unifying concepts from multiple disciplines, but should also involve various teaching strategies such as direct instruction, inquiry-based activities, and performance assessment opportunities. Interdisciplinary thematic units should culminate with students completing a presentation that allows them to summarise and show what they have learned. This variety in instructional techniques will create multiple opportunities for diverse learners to learn and demonstrate their knowledge.

**Supported inquiry-based teaching**

Supported inquiry-based teaching provides students with concrete learning experiences in a structured environment, increasing the meaningfulness of the information being learned while reducing language and literacy demands.

In an inquiry-based classroom, students are active participants in their own learning. The teacher spends minimal time lecturing and a maximum amount of time facilitating discussions and small-group activities. While moving about the room to observe students' work, the teacher often stops to talk with students one-on-one. Instead of giving answers, he asks questions to prompt and guide students' critical thinking and understanding. Students also contribute to the decisionmaking process.

Teachers will want to know how and when to use a variety of strategies within an inquiry-based pedagogy to increase students' understanding of core concepts and to enhance their reasoning and problem-solving skills. In practice, inquiry-based teaching typically occurs on a continuum. Depending on the teaching goal, teachers will move along the continuum, choosing strategies and activities that are most appropriate for the content.

At one end of the continuum is structured inquiry, where students might engage in a hands-on activity and draw conclusions, but follow precise instructions from the teacher. In the middle is guided inquiry, where. students might determine a procedure for the investigation, but the teacher chooses the question to be investigated and the materials to be used. Farther along the continuum is student- directed inquiry, in which students generate their own questions concerning a topic selected by the teacher, and design their own investigation.

At the start of an inquiry-based lesson, teachers will want to determine all students' prior knowledge and possible misconceptions about the topic to be investigated. If students are not familiar with the subject, teachers can provide general information or engage students in introductory experiences with the material prior to the activity. Teachers will want to be sure that students know what they're looking for in a structured inquiry activity.

During questioning, teachers will want to be sure to call on students with learning disabilities as often as they call on students without disabilities. Students should be given ample time to respond to questions and teachers should not interrupt or redirect too soon, but work to improve students' responses by prompting students or rephrasing the question. Teachers should respond to questions or statements from students with learning disabilities as thoroughly and with as much positive affect as they would respond to other students.

Science activities alone may not be enough to help students with learning disabilities learn essential vocabulary. Though vocabulary learning is sometimes minimised in hands-on science activities, students must still master key vocabulary used in classroom discussion. Vocabulary words can be presented by the teacher or practiced in a peer tutoring format in which students paraphrase or summarise what they have read after paragraph or page.

Students can be encouraged to write down vocabulary as it is encountered and refer to the glossary of their textbook. They can also create a vocabulary index by writing new words on a separate index card, arranging the cards alphabetically, and placing them on a ring so that new words can be added as needed.

Mnemonic (memory-enhancing) techniques can be effective in helping students with learning disabilities to learn scientific vocabulary. These techniques typically employ familiar, concrete, visual, and auditory cues to help students remember words and definitions.

For teachers who want to address the learning needs of individual students, this is an essential teaching skill. It helps if teachers understand how mathematics is organised as a discipline. Sometimes, modifications need to be made quickly. Teachers can be in the middle of a unit, or even in the middle of a conversation, and realize that some students need extra support or a different approach.

If a teacher suspects that modifications will be necessary for some students, she will want to plan ahead. To help students develop their reasoning and problem-solving skills, teachers will want to design curriculum around big ideas or central concepts that can facilitate learning of subordinate concepts. Understanding big ideas in mathematics enables students to solve diverse problems which may appear to be unrelated but are, in fact, connected in some way to a larger mathematical concept.

Big ideas in mathematics contain many concepts. Teachers can organise big ideas and subordinate concepts into strands which can be taught over a number of days. Strands make the sequencing of concepts more manageable for many students, especially students with learning disabilities who can be overwhelmed if too many concepts are taught too quickly.

Problem solving can be difficult to teach, yet it is one of the most important areas in mathematics instruction because it affects nearly every aspect of a person's life. The ability to problem solve is as crucial for students with learning disabilities as it is for all other students. However, students with learning disabilities often need explicit instruction in the strategies of problem solving and guided learning experiences in solving problems in mathematics.

Most interpretations of problem solving include the notion of confronting a situation that contains novel and challenging elements. When faced with such a situation, a person's problem solving occurs on two levels. One level is metacognitive: Which problem-solving strategy is most appropriate for a given problem situation? This question requires a person to analyse the situation, reflect on his prior knowledge, choose a strategy, apply it, and evaluate its effectiveness.

The other level involves applying the strategy— a specific approach to dealing with the problem, such as creating visual representations of problems, noticing patterns, or working a problem backward. The student with a learning disability will typically try many strategies to solve a problem, but the strategies may be ineffective or inefficient, such as rereading a problem or shifting computations. Even when students learn effective problem-solving strategies, it can be difficult for them to decide when and how to use a particular strategy in a new context.

The following are the tips for teaching problem solving:

i) Begin problem solving as part of the initial mathematics program. Do not wait.

ii) Make problem solving the reason for computation.

iii) Assist students with what they cannot do so that they can solve problems. If a student cannot read the problem, rewrite it. If the computation is too complex, break it down into smaller steps.

iv) Ask students to write their own problems and to modify existing problems.

v) Use familiar and culturally relevant subject matter as the content for the problems.

vi) Monitor progress and modify problems as necessary.

## References

Barnett, R., "Linking Teaching and Research", *Journal of Higher Education*, Vol. 63, No. 6, pp. 619-636, 1992.

Biggs, J.B., *Teaching for Quality Learning at University: What the Student Does, Open University Press*, Milton Keynes, 1999.

Bresler, J.B., "Teaching Effectiveness and Government Awards", *Science, Vol.160*, pp. 164-167, 1968.

Brew, A. & Boud, D., "Research and Learning in Higher Education", in Research, Teaching and Learning in Higher Education, eds B. Smith & S. Brown, Kogan Page, London, pp. 30-39, 1995.

Brew, A. & Boud, D., "Teaching and research: Establishing the Vital Link with Learning", *Higher Education*, Vol. 29, pp. 261-273, 1995.

Bley, N.S., Thornton, C.A., *Teaching mathematics to students with learning disabilities* (3rd ed.), Austin, TX: Pro-Ed, 1995.

Branca, N., Breedlove, B., King, B., "Calculators in the middle grades: Access to rich mathematics", In J.T. Fey & C.R. Hirsch (Eds.), *Calculators in mathematics education: 1992 yearbook*, Reston, VA: National Council of Teachers of Mathematics, 1992.

Dalton, B., Morocco, C.C., Tivnan, T., & Mead, P.L.R., "Supported inquiry science: Teaching for conceptual change in urban and suburban science classrooms", *Journal of Learning Disabilities, 30*(6), 670-684, 1997.

Finson, K.D., Ormsbee, C.K., "Rubrics and their use in inclusive science", *Intervention in School and Clinic, 34*(2), 79-88, 1998.

Kober, N., *Edtalk: What we know about science teaching and learning,* Washington, DC: Council for Educational Development and Research, 1991.

Lovitt, T.C., Horton, S.V., "Strategies for adapting science textbooks for youth with learning disabilities", *Remedial and Special Education, 15*(2), 105-116, 1994.

# 10

# Emerging Paradigm for Design-based Research

Design-based research is an emerging paradigm for the study of learning in context through the systematic design and study of instructional strategies and tools. The design-based research can help create and extend knowledge about developing, enacting, and sustaining innovative learning environments. The phrase of design-based research methods is used deliberately to avoid invoking mistaken identification with experimental design, with studies of designers, or with trial teaching methods. The good design-based research exhibits the following five characteristics:

i) The central goals of designing learning environments and developing theories or "prototheories" of learning are intertwined.

ii) Development and research take place through continuous cycles of design, enactment, analysis, and redesign.

iii) Research on designs must lead to sharable theories that help communicate relevant implications to practitioners and other educational designers.

iv) Research must account for how designs function in authentic settings. It must not only document success or failure but also focus on interactions that refine our understanding of the learning issues involved.

v) The development of such accounts relies on methods that can document and connect processes of enactment to outcomes of interest.

The last few years have seen a renewed effort to close the "credibility gap" in educational research. Some see this gap as arising from unscientific research approaches, while others point to the detachment of research from practice. Educational research that is detached from practice may not account for the influence of contexts, the emergent and complex nature of outcomes, and the incompleteness of knowledge about which factors are relevant for prediction.

Claiming success for an educational intervention is a tricky business. If success means being certain that an intervention caused learning, then we need to look carefully at the intervention in a particular setting. Design-based research methods focus on designing and exploring the whole range of designed innovations: artifacts as well as less concrete aspects such as activity structures, institutions, scaffolds, and curricula. Importantly, design-based research goes beyond merely designing and testing particular interventions.

Interventions embody specific theoretical claims about teaching and learning, and reflect a commitment to understanding the relationships among theory, designed artifacts, and practice. At the same time, research on specific interventions can contribute to theories of learning and teaching.

Design-based research methods respond to emergent features of the setting. For example, the Passion School Project articulated theoretical principles that should drive an interest-based curriculum, including the principle that students develop competencies in adult-defined learning objectives through engagement in authentic work in their area of interest. Micro-analyses of student interactions with activities based on that principle enabled redesign and refinement of activities, and ultimately refinement of the underlying interest-driven learning framework.

Thus, emergent behaviours of students in response to activities drove development of the intervention and development of theory. These developments would have been unimaginable in the absence of real student choices. Finally, in design-based research, practitioners and researchers work together to produce meaningful change in contexts of practice (e.g., classrooms, after-school programmes, teacher online communities). Such collaboration means that goals and design constraints are drawn from the local context as well as the researcher's agenda, addressing one concern of many reform efforts.

Engaging such partnerships across multiple settings can uncover relationships between the numerous variables that come into play in classroom contexts and help refine the key components of an intervention. In particular, these partnerships can help us distinguish between a "lethal mutation"—a reinterpretation that no longer captures the pedagogical essence of the innovation—from a productive adaptation—a reinterpretation that preserves this essence, but tailors the activity to the needs and characteristics of particular classrooms.

Design-based research has recently been described as a potentially fruitful methodology for generating causal accounts of learning and instruction that could form the basis for systematic, randomised clinical trials. The design-based research as raising important questions for research applied to practice and for research methods, generally. The use of randomised trials may hinder innovation studies by prematurely judging the efficacy of an intervention. Additionally, randomised trials may systematically fail to account for phenomena that violate this method's basic assumptions—that is, phenomena that are contextually dependent or those that result from the interaction of dozens, if not hundreds, of factors.

Indeed, such phenomena are precisely what educational research most needs to account for in order to have application to educational practice. The design-based research can generate plausible causal accounts because of its focus on linking processes to outcomes in particular settings, and can productively be linked with controlled laboratory experiments or randomised clinical trials by assisting in the identification of relevant contextual factors, aiding in identification of mechanisms, and enriching our understanding of the nature of the intervention itself.

The design-based research differs from evaluation research in the ways context and interventions are problematised. In traditional evaluation, an "intervention"—an instructional program, a textbook, or a policy—is measured against a set of standards. During formative evaluation, iterative cycles of development, implementation, and study allow the designer to gather information about how an intervention is or is not succeeding in ways that might lead to better design. Then the intervention is "frozen," and the rigorous summative evaluation begins. Evaluators often conceptualise context as a set of factors that are independent of the intervention itself but that may influence its effects.

Like formative evaluation, design-based research uses mixed methods to analyse an intervention's outcomes and refine the intervention. Unlike evaluation research, design-based research views a successful innovation as a joint product of the designed intervention and the context. Hence, design-based research goes beyond perfecting a particular product. The intention of design-based research in education is to inquire more broadly into the nature of learning in a complex system and to refine generative or predictive theories of learning. Models of successful innovation can be generated through such work-models, rather than particular artifacts or programmes, are the goal.

The commitment to using theory-driven design to generate complex interventions that can be improved through empirical study and that can contribute to more basic understanding of the underlying theory raises significant challenges. Objectivity, reliability, and validity are all necessary to make design-based research a scientifically sound enterprise, but these qualities are managed in noticeably different ways than in controlled experimentation.

Design-based research relies on techniques used in other research paradigms, like thick descriptive datasets, systematic analysis of data with carefully defined measures, and consensus building within the field around interpretations of data. By trying to promote objectivity while attempting to facilitate the intervention, design-based researchers regularly find themselves in the dual intellectual roles of advocate and critic. In particular, design-based research typically triangulates multiple sources and kinds of data to connect intended and unintended outcomes to processes of enactment.

Complications arise from sustained intervention in messy settings. A single, complex intervention might involve hundreds, if not thousands, of discrete designer, researcher, and teacher decisions—hopefully working in concert—in an attempt to promote innovative practice. In these situations, causality can be difficult to decipher and dis-ambiguate; all possible factors cannot logistically be equally pursued; precise replication of an intervention is largely impossible; and emergent phenomena regularly lead to new lines of inquiry informed by current theories or models of the phenomena.

Reliability of findings and measures can be promoted through triangulation from multiple data sources, repetition of analyses across cycles of enactment, and use (or creation) of standardised measures or instruments. Validity of findings is often addressed by the partnerships and iteration typical of design-based research, which result in increasing alignment of theory, design, practice, and measurement over time.

A logistical challenge for design-based researchers involves maintaining a productive collaborative partnership with participants in the research context. Since a single line of research often investigates multiple cycles of design, enactment, and study, the work can span years and touch on closely held commitments of the researchers and teachers.

Indeed, successful examples of design-based research often are conducted within a single setting over a long time, and the success of the innovation and the knowledge gained from its study depend in part on being able to sustain the partnership between researchers and teachers. There is a trade-off here between the refinement of a particular innovation to maximise its success, and the generalisation of findings from an ultimately highly refined enactment.

The value of design-based research should be measured by its ability to improve educational practice. There are four areas where design-based research methods provide the most promise:

i) exploring possibilities for creating novel learning and teaching environments,
ii) developing theories of learning and instruction that are contextually based,
iii) advancing and consolidating design knowledge, and
iv) increasing capacity for educational innovation.

Efforts to design, use, and do research on educational tools and materials in real settings can promote the adoption of innovations. They can help researchers and designers understand the real-world demands placed on designs and on adopters of designs. In addition, pursuing development and enactment through close collaboration with teachers places them in direct ownership of designs.

Design-based research can contribute to such theories through rich accounts of instructional interventions and their effects across multiple settings and in multiple areas of instruction. Design-based research can lead to an understanding of relevant design knowledge and practices as they apply to naturalistic settings. In design-oriented fields, design knowledge is often characterised by common examples, patterns, and principles, and by the expertise required to apply these generalities in specific settlings.

Currently, design-based research communicates this knowledge in many forms, including narratives of planned and enacted instruction, design principles connecting enacted designs to educational outcomes of interest, and design patterns abstracted from one or more settings describing how a designed innovation interacts with settings and evolves. Design-based research provides numerous opportunities for the exchange of expertise across disciplinary boundaries.

## Design-based Research for Effective Technology Education

Focusing on technology use still leaves open the issue of what the technology is being used for. The wide range of technology applications includes such simple activities as learning to type on a computer keyboard or using the internet to look up the meanings of words, to such complex applications as virtual simulations. Appealing to the need for improving student achievement helps narrow the range of technology applications to be considered: the applications should be those that can logically be linked to enhanced achievement.

For example, technology applications that support students with particular learning issues, such as students having difficulty learning to read or students learning English as their second language, may merit special consideration. Socio-economic levels are another factor to consider.

An important consideration in the design of a large scale study investigating technology's impact on student learning is to consider the ways in which technologies can be used to support academic learning at different grade-levels and across different content areas. With the growth of networked, multimedia technologies a number of technology-based learning programmes now combine application types. Programmes like Adventures in Supercomputing, for example, use a mix of technologies to introduce high school students to the field of computational science. Students engage in long-term projects that require them to pose hypotheses and devise methods and procedures for solving problems. They use a range of technology resources including online information, graphing and modeling tools, and email to communicate with professional scientists who serve as mentors.

The goal behind such initiatives is to support students in solving complex problems employing methods, procedures, and strategies that mirror those used by discipline experts. At the middle and high school levels students are much more likely to be using productivity tools, as well as problem-solving software, and information resources. Computers and the internet are relatively common fixtures in schools. The availability of standalone instructional software varies by grade level, with generally more tool-based applications (such as word processing and spreadsheets) becoming increasingly more prevalent by secondary school.

The effectiveness of specific educational technology interventions has been studied across a wide range of content areas, grade levels, and type of student. The study of educational technology interventions provides a number of challenges in this regard:

i) Both the quantity and variety of technologies in schools continue to increase;
ii) Educational technology interventions are not typically stable over time (i.e., new versions of software replace older versions; more powerful computer processors come to market; multimedia and graphical displays increase in resolution and become more interactive; new tools obviate or change the patterns of use of old ones; etc.)
iii) Uptodate information on the prevalence of uses of specific educational technology interventions is not generally available; and
vi) A substantial period of time—often stretching over years—is required to conduct and publish a single high-quality study.

## REFERENCES

Ayersman, D., "Reviewing the research on hypermedia-based learning", *Journal of Research on Computing in Education*, 28:4, 500-525, 1996.

Bayraktar, S., "A Meta-analysis of the effectiveness of computer-assisted instruction in science education", *Journal of Research on Technology in Education* 34:3, 173-188, 2002.

Berson, M., "Effectiveness of computer technology in the social studies: A Review of the literature", *Journal of Research on Computing in Education*, 28:4, 486-499, 1996.

Blok, H., Oostdam, R., Otter, M. and Overmaat, M., "Computer-assisted instruction in support of beginning reading instruction: A review", *Review of Educational Research*, 72:1, 101-130, 2002.

Dynarski, Mark, Margaret Honey, Doug Levin, "Designing A Study of the Effectiveness of Education Technology", *Background Material for the First Meeting of the Technical Working Group*, 1996.

Fitzgerald, G. and Koury, K., "Empirical advances in technology-assisted instruction for students with mild and moderate disabilities", *Journal of Research on Computing in Education*, 28:4, 526-553, 1996.

Hennessy, S., *The potential of portable technologies for supporting graphing investigations*, Institute of Educational Technology, Open University, UK, 1998.

Jones, T. and Paolucci, R., "The learning effectiveness of educational technology: A call for further research", *Educational Technology Review,* 9:10-14,1998

Lee, J., "Effectiveness of computer-based instructional simulation: A meta-analysis", *International Journal of Instructional Media,* 26:1, 71-85, 1999.

Liu, M., Moore, Z., Graham, L., and Lee, S., "A look at the research on computer-based technology use in second-language learning: A review of the literature from 1990-2000", *Journal of Research on Technology in Education* 34:3, 250-273, 2002.

Reed, W.M., "Assessing the impact of computer-based writing instruction", *Journal of Research on Computing in Education,* 28:4, 418-437, 1996.

Weller, H., "Assessing the impact of computer-based learning in science", *Journal of Research on Computing in Education* 28:4, 461-485, 1996.

# 11

# Multicultural Curriculum Research

Multicultural incorporation throughout the teacher education curriculum can have as its culminating experience the "successful completion of student teaching contingent upon acceptable performance on multicultural criteria embedded in regular performance appraisal criteria and procedures". The anti-bias/anti-racist aims of multicultural education are advanced by the skilled culturally responsive teacher who is able to transform a conventional curriculum.

A teacher education programme may reasonably expect a student teacher to attempt to transform a mainstream curriculum or at least include multicultural content that works toward anti-bias/anti-racist goals. A teacher education programme can engage preservice teachers in an interrogation of the actual enactment of the curriculum and how the socially constructed belief systems and identities of teachers mediate the organisation and content of their teaching.

Increased multicultural content coherence throughout programmes tied to student teaching performance criteria increases both the potential for the clarity of expectations and the realm of possibilities for multicultural content incorporation by future teachers in their field placements. Traditional classroom management expectations can be redesigned from a democratic, multicultural perspective.

Without the knowledge base and skills in designing meaningful instructional units informed by a transformative multicultural perspective, future teachers may flounder in field experiences designed to demonstrate competency in multicultural content integration. From the first contact of preservice teachers with a programme and continuing through their student teaching internship, a programme must constantly reflect and reinforce multicultural knowledge, dispositions, and skills.

Multicultural or intercultural education has for quite a long time been a topic of discussion among professionals who work with children of ethnic minorities. Recently, the concept of intercultural education in a multicultural society has been gaining a wider audience. To some, multicultural education seems to be an additional subject that should be introduced into the school curriculum. To others, it is rather a life style with underlying principles that can and should be implemented in any educational situation.

Some approaches suffer from political naivety or turn out to bear a sophisticated hidden potential for the assimilation and political neutralisation of minority groups. Others are used by fundamentalist minority organisations and right-wing majority groups alike to plead for segregation for the sake of maintenance of cultural identity.

Teachers who were accustomed to talking about children's progress in class felt insecure about how to react when parents started to discuss their family problems. Sometimes they felt it was difficult to integrate their newly gained insights into the living conditions of children and parents, or they felt that the responsibility for unfamiliar problems was more than they could cope with. The process brought about the necessity to exchange views and cooperate with colleagues in other fields of work who were likely to look at a problem from a different angle and come to different conclusions.

The professional's potential for cultural arrogance is high and by no means limited to those working in the formal system. The tendency of professionals to display cultural arrogance can be intentional, but often it is not. It can be based on consciously assuming that one knows better because of one's vocational background; often it isn't. It can be due to the quality of the professional's vocational training or the degree to which the professional is unconscious of his or her motives and capacities. Unfortunately, it is often reinforced by the need for constant self-adulation, and by the success-seeking that results from a lack of job security.

## Responsive Teaching Approach

Research suggests that early childhood curricula should provide opportunities for children to interact with peers, caregivers, and aspects of their environment, and to engage in active rather than passive activities. Caregivers must be continually responsive to the spontaneously expressed interests and intentions of children as they pursue informal activities. Moreover, to sufficiently meet the needs of children from diverse cultural backgrounds, teaching practices must be relevant to, and meaningful in, the sociocultural context of the systems in which children live and develop.

Evidence from research suggests, however, that children from diverse backgrounds do not all interact in the same ways with adults in classroom activities. Responsive teaching occurs when caregivers offer sensitive guidance and assistance at points in "the zone of proximal development" at which children require assistance. Responsive teaching involves the construction and negotiation of shared meaning or perspective in conversational interaction.

Intersubjectivity, the linguistic concept denoting a sharing of purpose or focus in the coordination of perspectives, is crucial in responsive teaching because it is important for collaborative partners to determine a common ground for communication and understanding. Within this context, children actively participate in the construction of knowledge, and as a result, gain an increasingly advanced understanding of the skills and perspectives of their culture.

Responsive teaching is predicated on the interactive patterns between adults and children observed in many cultures, and in joint activity settings where participants have different skills and skill levels. It differs from conventionally defined means of instruction in several ways. First, responsive teaching should not be conceptualised as the simple transfer of knowledge and skills by those knowing more to those knowing less. Both adult and child collaborate in structuring the situations that provide the latter with opportunities to observe and participate in culturally valued activities, thereby enabling children to extend their skills and knowledge to a higher level of competence.

Therefore, unlike conventional instructive practices, responsive teaching does not assist children in developing skills they do not already possess; rather, it "rouses to life" those functions and skills that are in the process of maturing. Second, traditional or teacher-directed forms of instruction involve making presuppositions about a task explicitly known prior to task engagement. This minimises the child's active role in constructing understanding of the task, while maximising the teacher's role.

In responsive teaching, however, the teacher's role is to provide just enough guidance to enable the child, through his or her own efforts, to assume full control in performing a task. Third, teacher-directed instruction typically employs a single teaching method. While the goal of education should not be to produce children who have the same talents and abilities, many outcomes with respect to knowledge, skills, and dispositions should be the same for all children. Responsive teaching, therefore, involves the systematic use of a repertoire of alternative strategies that are more likely to be suitable to children having diverse needs and learning styles.

Responsive teaching methods should not be confused with accelerated attempts to teach academic skills to preschool children. In short, responsive teaching helps children to:

i) build bridges between what they already know and what they are capable of knowing;

ii) structure and support their efforts in interesting and meaningful activities; and

iii) assume increasing responsibility for task performance and management.

Children increase their understanding by relating what they are learning to what they already know. This bridging between the known and the new in communicative interaction presumes intersubjectivity. Thus, in dealing with culturally diverse children, initial differences in perspective must be modified in order to reach a common ground for communication.

Multicultural Education addresses the dimensions of curricular content integration, knowledge construction, prejudice reduction, an equity pedagogy, and the creation of empowering school cultures. Contemporary multicultural education emerged from the civil rights era of the 1950s and 1960s when the effects of racism were a central political reason for social action. Ending racism was a primary impetus from which the civil rights movement and, subsequently, multicultural education reform originated.

For these reasons multicultural education draws from an historical foundation of exclusions and holds as a priority rectifying the exclusionary effects of racism. Furthermore, how a predominately white teaching force conservatively interprets multicultural dimensions places a mighty challenge before the teacher education community.

To deepen multicultural education, teacher educators can examine the entire range of programme multicultural content integration by engaging with their colleagues in contextually based self-studies and internal programme evaluations to assess the coherence among social foundations and psychology courses, methodology sequences, and student teaching. Ladson-Billings explains, "Multicultural teacher education occupies a critical position between multicultural theory and multicultural practice". Theoretical programme conceptual frameworks that envision culturally responsive teachers can be assessed by teacher candidate performances.

Institutional self-assessments can determine specific approaches within a programme's curriculum that teacher candidates actually use for multicultural curriculum development and instruction. Using both formative and summative assessments, goals for incorporating programme multicultural content can then be compared contextually to actual programme practices. Content integration or incorporation is one area that can be an accessible starting point for multicultural education reform within teacher education programmes.

## CONTEXTUAL TEACHING AND LEARNING (CTL)

Contextual teaching and learning (CTL) can provide a teacher education programme a pedagogical opportunity for addressing multicultural education dimensions. CTL can help teacher candidates connect more directly with culturally diverse communities where children and youth live and attend school.

Efforts to articulate CTL as a distinct educational approach have been elusive, mainly because it is an amalgam of several practical and philosophical orientations, including experiential learning, authentic instruction, work-based learning, service-learning, and applied learning, to name a few.

Recently, some general guidelines have been put forth toward helping teacher educators and educational practitioners with CTL implementation, which is an important first step. However, in order for full implementation of CTL to be realised, practitioners are going to need more specific means to guide their planning, direction and evaluation activities.

CTL is both a philosophy of education and a continuum of pedagogical strategies. As a philosophy of education it assumes that an educator's role is to help students find meaning in their education by making connections between what they are learning in the classroom and ways in which that knowledge can be applied in the world. It is intended to help students understand why what they are learning is important. CTL instructional strategies incorporate techniques that help students become more actively engaged as learners and reflective about their experiences.

Contextual learning occurs when students apply and experience what is being taught by referencing real problems and needs associated with their roles and responsibilities as family members, citizens, students, and workers. Contextual Teaching and Learning (CTL) emphasises higher-level thinking, knowledge transfer across academic disciplines, and collecting, analysing and synthesising information and data from multiple sources and viewpoints.

Contextual learning is not a new idea. CTL is not just rooted in philosophy it is also biologically compatible. Recent research on understanding how the brain functions has shed light on the importance of making connections in what we learn. In the 1970's a popular term used for CTL was experiential learning.

There are six elements were identified as important for CTL. These are:

i) Meaningful learning,
ii) Application of knowledge,
iii) Higher-order thinking,
iv) Standards-related curriculum,
v) Cultural-responsiveness, and
vii) Authentic assessment.

Each of these six elements, except for standards-based and cultural-responsiveness, has been addressed in the frameworks for CTL. These six elements are inter-related.

*Meaningful learning*: The understanding, personal relevance and valuing that a learner attaches to the content of what is to be learned. Learning is perceived as relevant to their lives. Without emphasis on creating meaning for learners, many students will avoid learning the desired content because they see it as irrelevant to their lives. Research has found the lack of perceived relevance to be one of the major contributors to students dropping out of school.

*Application of Knowledge*: The ability to see how what is learned applies to other settings and functions in the present or future. The application of knowledge is the most commonly used strategy in CTL for helping studentscreate meaning in what is learned. Students are seldom interested in abstract learning that is not connected to the real world.

*Higher order thinking*: The learner is required to use critical and creative thinking in collecting data, understanding an issue, or solving a problem. The use of higher order thinking helps develop the mind and skills of the learner as well as contribute to a deeper understanding of what is learned. Without it, students may quickly forget what has merely been memorised for a test.

*Standards-related curricula*: The content of the instruction relates to a range and variety of local, state, national, association and/or industry standards. Curricula based on agreed upon standards provide a strong rationale for what is taught in specific classes and at various grade levels. It provides a stronger framework for articulated content across grade levels than relying on the personal preferences or experiences of individual teachers.

*Cultural Responsiveness*: Educators must understand and respect the values, beliefs, and customs of our students, fellow educators, and the community in which we educate. A variety of individual and group cultures influence learning. These cultures, and the relationship among these cultures, affect how educators teach. At least four perspectives should be considered: the individual learner, groups of learners (such as teams or an entire classroom), the school setting, and the larger community setting. Teachers who are sensitive to differences in culture not only adjust their instructional strategies to fit differences in individual student's cultures and language experiences but also adjust to differences in various school and community environments.

*Authentic assessment*: This is use of multiple assessment strategies that validly reflect the actual outcomes expected of the learner. These can include assessment of student projects and activities, use.of portfolios, rubrics, checklists, and observation guides as well as having students become active participants in assessing their own learning and using each assessment to improve their learning.

Authentic assessment merges instruction and evaluation in a naturalistic way that reflects both the content of what is to be learned as well as the applications of such knowledge.

To teach for meaning and application and then assess only for memory of facts creates dissonance in students and teachers alike.

**Authenticity Assessment in CTL**

Authenticity in learning is based on the premise that its demonstration must be through experiences with, and performance in the real world. That is, to have personal value, generate interest and produce functional knowledge and skills, the act of learning must be in the context of, and directly relevant to the knowledge, skills and performances expected by the community at large. Authenticity is part of the underlying foundation of contextual teaching and learning, particularly as to how learning is assessed. Authentic assessment is an indivisible element of the contextual teaching and learning process.

Authentic assessment can best be distinguished from traditional modes of educational assessment by qualities that foster formative development of teaching and learning processes. And it is through this distinction, that fundamental aims of contextual teaching and learning are advanced by authentic assessment, which:

a) Entails a pedagogical shift toward application, analysis, and synthesis that occurs in contextual teaching and learning;
b) Employs assessment tasks that are "real instances" of extended criterion performances of actual learning goals;
c) Involves students in in-depth situations in which they develop and habitually apply problem solving and higher-order thinking;
d) Entails collaboration between students and teachers to determine meaning and produce knowledge;
e) Includes multiple opportunities for students to learn and practice the desired outcomes, along with multiple opportunities for feedback and reflection;

f) Aims students toward producing discourse, products and performances that they value beyond school success;
g) Utilises rubrics and other criterion checklists at the core of authentic assessment as standards to improve learning and teaching;
h) Draws upon multiple sources of information over time and in multiple contexts, employing reflective use of journals, reflective essay writing, portfolios, applied performance exhibits, work samples, peer mirroring, action research, case studies, criterion checklists and the like;
i) Samples the actual integration of knowledge, skills, and dispositions desired of teachers as they are used in multiple kinds of pedagogical practice contexts.

Benefits resulting from a quantum investment in authentic assessment accrue both to the character of student learning, and to the pedagogic insights gained by teachers:

i) Encourages students to become engaged in problem solving and grounded in meaningful, real-life tasks that are incrementally more complex;
ii) Provides students are with multiple forms of evidence about their learning, and in so doing, to make connections between home and school, and come to value the learning process as well as the product;
iii) Allows students to gain greater clarity about their obligations and what they are expected to master;
iv) Enables students to utilise knowledge effectively and employ disciplined inquiry to answer questions that are relevant to their lives and their communities;
v) Results in more equitable educational outcomes for girls and children of color;
vi) Enhances the ability of teachers to see assessment results as meaningful and useful for improving instruction;

vii) Encourages teachers to change the way they think about knowledge, instruction, and academic success;

viii) Refines teachers' abilities to use multiple sources of evidence to assess students' performance.

**Issues in Teacher Preparation**

Contextual teaching and learning (CTL) is rooted in contextual teacher preparation (CTP). Teachers' concerns and practices relating to CTL fell into seven major categories:

i) Teacher Expectations

ii) Reflective Practice

iii) Political Issues

iv) Institutional Support

v) Curriculum Development Versus Curriculum Manage*ment*

Teachers felt that a key factor in using CTL rested with being secure in its use. Such security rests partially in school support and partially in the thoroughness of teacher preparation. Teachers would like to be better at analysing problems. They felt it would have been helpful if they had entered teaching with experience in applying specific problem solving strategies. Peer coaching was valued during teacher preparation but it was largely absent in practice, and teachers felt they lacked useful alternatives.

Teachers wanted assistance with issues related to how to build a support base, get allies, interact with administrators and be effective advocates for CTL. They wanted more experience with classroom management. Teachers need more concerted preparation on teaching to concepts and learning processes rather than to content.

## References

Carter, K., "Using cases to frame mentor-novice conversations about teaching", *Theory Into Practice,* 27. 214-222/, 1989.

Everett, D., "Marketing education assessment guide", *Performance-based activities with authentic assessment instruments*, Columbia, MO: Missouri University, Instructional materials laboratory, 1997.

Gay, G., "Multicultural infusiou in teacher education, Foundations and applications", *Peabody Journal of Education*, 72(1), 150-177, 1997.

Smith Jr. Albert J., *Authentic Assessment Advances Contextual Teaching and Learning*, University of Washington Seattle, Washington, Talking Paper Series Paper #1.01, October, 2000

Terry, C., Pantle, T., "Authentic assessment: Reducing the fear and trembling", *ERIC Digest*, ERIC Clearinghouse on Tests, Measurement and Evaluation, Washington, D.C., 1994.

Vavrus, Michael, *The Multicultural Challenge of Racism and the Pedagogical Opportunity of Contextual Teaching & Learning*, 2001.

# 12

# Research on Effective Teaching

Effective teachers have good rapport with students and encourage their classroom involvement through verbal and non-verbal cues. The quick starters enjoy their teaching and their students, expressing positive and optimistic attitudes about the undergraduates on their campuses. The following are the characteristics of effective teaching:

i) The instructors get right down to business. They begin class promptly and are well organised.

ii) They teach at an appropriately fast pace, but stop regularly to check student comprehension and engagement.

iii) They use a variety of instructional strategies rather than lecture alone.

iv) They focus on the topic and their instructional objectives and do not get sidetracked. Their explanations are clear.

v) They use humour that is in keeping with their individual styles.

vi) They practise good classroom management techniques, holding the attention and respect of the group.

vii) They interact with students by providing immediate answers to questions or comments and corrective feedback when needed. They appreciate students' answers and used probing questions to extend the answers.

viii) They provide a cordial climate by allowing students to speak freely and include personal humour or other attempts to relate to students as people.

ix) They use nonverbal behaviour, such as gestures, walking around and eye contact to reinforce their comments.

Joseph Lowman describes the following as the two main dimensions of effective college teaching:

i) Intellectual excitement (enthusiasm, knowledge, inspiration, humour, interesting viewpoint, clarity, organisation), and

ii) Interpersonal concern/Effective motivation.

They can, and have been, identified by researchers, students and professionals alike. Inspection of these characteristics fails to support another commonly held belief about teaching: good instructors are born, not made. While certain characteristics such as humour and interpersonal skills seem to come easily to some people and not others, people are not born with knowledge of a given discipline or competency in the use of instructional strategies. Furthermore, those who exhibit these qualities most consistently state that they work hard at attaining them and are very conscious of their actions and their effects.

Most instructors often carry on the process without a great deal of conscious attention, and rather unsystematically. What distinguish those who learn best, however, are the very level of conscious reflection and the quality of information they bring to bear in determining the effects of a practice in a particular context. The best instructors know not only what they are doing, but also why it is working and why it is likely to work in one kind of environment and not in another. Although they may have some natural personality characteristics that support their success, they also work very hard at their teaching and continually try to improve.

A number of writers have observed differences in style among instructors. They classify them according to a number of dimensions that represent how the instructors approach their students, the ways in which they think learning takes place, and personal strengths and preferences. Lowman, for example, observes that exemplary college instructors "appear to be those who are highly proficient in either one of two fundamental sets of skills: the ability to offer presentations in clearly organised and interesting ways (intellectual excitement) or to relate to students in ways that communicate positive regard and motivate them to work hard to meet academic challenges. All are probably at least completely competent in both sets of skills, but outstanding in one or, occasionally, even both of them."

The following are the five effective teaching styles:

i) *Expert:* Concerned with transmitting information from an expert status; challenges students to enhance their competence.
ii) *Formal authority:* Concerned with the acceptable ways to do things and providing students with the structure they need to learn.
iii) *Personal model:* Believes in teaching by personal example; oversees and guides students to emulate.
iv) *Facilitator:* Emphasises the personal nature of instructor-student interactions; guides students toward developing their capacity for independent action.
v) *Delegator:* Concerned with developing students' capacity to function autonomously; encourages independent projects.

Sustaining growth in teaching involves continuing to learn. A model of teaching development rooted in experiential learning, suggests that experienced instructors can avoid burnout and continue to improve through:

i) stimulating their thinking by taking advantage of opportunities to learn of new approaches to teaching through reading.

ii) attending workshops and conferences, observing colleagues and joining book groups or seminars on teaching topics.

iii) relying on colleagues or teaching consultants to provide them support as they experiment with teaching or to challenge them to try new things.

iv) obtaining regular, systematic feedback on their teaching and making changes based on that feedback.

v) reflecting on their teaching continually and making changes based on those reflections.

The challenging task of being the kind of instructor who continually strives to improve instructional technique is approached by instructors who are simultaneously conducting their own studies or research programme as well as engaging in service activities and maintaining a personal life. Often, instructors feel caught among all these roles and have the sense that they aren't performing up to their personal standards. Severe stress can result.

A major instructional goal in many courses is to develop students' ability to work with problems in the discipline. Teachers are responsible for transmitting two levels of knowledge to their students. First, and by far the most important, they need to explain how a member of the discipline perceives the situation and brings order to a maze of raw data. By this time teachers have taken a substantial number of courses in the discipline and have internalised the discipline's perspective on the world. In contrast, the students are just beginning to learn the material and might have a naive—that is to say, a non-disciplinary view of the problem. Second, teachers need to explain how these general principles apply to the specific case covered by a particular problem.

An appropriate teaching technique might involve demonstrating a problem's solution by systematically explaining the rationale for every step in a solution. Alternatively, teachers may opt for more active participation by their students and ask members of the class to take the lead and explain how they perceive the problem. Still greater student participation can be achieved by dividing the class into small groups and having group members take turns in leading a discussion on solving the problem.

The group's solutions can then be checked in a general classwide session. A little practice will help to decide which technique works best for the course content to be covered and for the kind of students in the class. One way to help students clarify their assumptions is to quiz them after they have read the material related to the problem. Teachers might ask questions which require students to restate the givens of the problem; they might ask for a restatement of the problem's goal; or they might try to diagnose their reading of individual sentences within the problem by asking students to represent each sentence based on pictures, flowcharts, equations, or other metaphors.

Another aspect of teaching problem representation involves asking students to bring the facts and assumptions together to characterise or categorise the problem. This can help to better explain to the students what they want them to know or do. Useful strategies to help students state the problem include: helping students separate relevant and irrelevant information and representing the problem in another form. When students have adequately represented the problem and examined their assumptions, they next need to develop a solution plan.

To assist students in developing such a solution plan, teachers need to know what general model or procedure students have in mind for solving the problem. This is the point where students synthesise their relevant information and definitions to generate a solution plan for this particular problem. Useful strategies include: setting sub-goals; identifying necessary operations; and describing the interlocking steps of the argument, and drawing conclusions. These procedures and computation skills can be enhanced by practice in using different kinds of evidence to see which is most persuasive or by practising calculations.

## Professional Development

Today, teachers remain engaged in many different types of professional development, ranging from workshops offered in their schools or districts to professional conferences and summer institutes. Through the varied sources of professional development, teachers report participating in a wide range of professional development activities. Other popular forms of professional development include independent professional reading and working on a school or district committee on a topic related to curriculum and instruction.

Changes in teachers' professional development activities over time reflect changes in the educational policy environment. In addition to understanding the many different types of professional development teachers are participating in, it is also important to assess the quality of their learning experiences. The research on professional development indicates that high-quality teacher training focuses on content, connects teachers' learning to their experiences in schools, and fosters dialogue and professional collaboration among teachers around instructional and pedagogical issues. In the past, however, professional development rarely reflected these characteristics.

More often than not, professional development is short-lived and episodic, unconnected to teachers' workplaces, and indifferent to teachers' prior experiences. Further, the number of teachers reporting that their professional development involve a series of single events with little or no follow-up has decreased significantly. Although more teachers are participating in professional development that reflects characteristics of quality, almost one-third of teachers are still participating in one-shot workshops, and fewer than half report that professional development meets their needs. Thus, while there is a positive trend toward more professional development with characteristics of quality, the percentage of teachers participating in such professional development is still relatively low.

The two forms of school-based professional development—coaching and collaborative work time—can exhibit many of the characteristics of effective professional development when implemented in supportive school contexts. At the school sites, the coaches perform a variety of tasks, including demonstrating lessons, observing teachers and providing feedback, and compiling student assessment data. Overall, the coaching appears to be a popular and effective professional development strategy, particularly at the elementary and middle school levels. The training works well because it is site specific, is tailored to the teachers' needs, and comes from people who know the curriculum and the particular challenges encountered by teachers and students.

Participation in coaching depends on the willingness of the teacher to accept support. When teachers feel least threatened by others observing their classrooms, coaching realises the greatest success. Beginning teachers tend to request and receive support, although more in the area of classroom management than for instructional assistance. Experienced teachers, meanwhile, are often reluctant to invite others to observe their classrooms or to heed the advice of coaches, especially if the guidance comes from people with few years of teaching experience.

In addition to coaching, some schools have dedicated time in their weekly schedules to enable collaborative work around instruction within grades and departments or for entire faculties. These schools have established minimum days, early-release days, delayed starts, or other creative scheduling to make time for faculty meetings or staff development. Again, this form of professional development occurs at all school levels—elementary, middle, and high.

Formal and informal teacher-initiated professional development earn high praise because of its focus and direct relevance to the needs of teachers. "The value of these informal sessions is twofold," an urban high school teacher said. Another measure of effectiveness is the extent to which professional development meets teachers' needs.

**Impact of Professional Development**

Greater percentages of teachers report that their professional development contribute "somewhat" to their development, a lower standard of effectiveness. Although teachers report only moderate impacts overall, many teachers are able to identify specific training activities that they feel contribute to their professional growth. Both new and experienced teachers appreciate instructional strategies or materials that they could use immediately in their classrooms. Teachers also benefited from relearning strategies. Some teachers add new strategies to their repertoire after observing colleagues and sharing instructional practices.

The policy environment for districts and schools has changed over the past several years, bringing a push for increased coherence of professional development, curriculum, and accountability. With the adoption of state standards in core academic subjects, there is increased emphasis on the content covered by teachers. To accommodate the focus on standards and accountability, however, the breadth of professional development has narrowed, both in the types of activities supported and in the content areas covered. As a result, professional development serves the needs of some schools and teachers while overlooking the needs of others.

According to teachers, curriculum alignment has produced mixed results for themselves and their students. Teachers are more familiar with what to teach but have not spent time focusing on how to teach the content effectively. While the type of professional development activities has narrowed to curriculum alignment, the number of subject areas addressed has also decreased. According to the administration, the school had implemented a comprehensive professional development plan designed to promote student achievement through standards-based instruction.

Although restricting the breadth of professional development may allow teachers to channel their energies and efforts into improving mathematics and language arts achievement, the winnowing of choices comes with costs to curricular diversity and teacher growth. Those subjects, science and social science, in particular, not tested at each grade level become victims in this educational triage. At one urban middle school, for example, to enable its language arts teachers to give more attention to literacy, the administration shifted the teaching of social science to the science and math teachers. The school, however, provided no additional professional development to prepare these teachers for the extra duties. Thus, as the focus of professional development narrows because of increased attention to standards and accountability, the needs of some teachers are neglected.

Even when strong professional development models are adopted by schools, the implementation of these models can be affected by the school context. Under the best circumstances, coaching and collaborative work time present meaningful learning opportunities to teachers. However, the realities of school workplace conditions can diminish the value of these professional development strategies. For example, the quality of the coaching can be affected by such aspects of working conditions as the coaches' years of teaching experience.

At hard-to-staff schools, the lack of teaching experience in the faculty as a whole is also reflected in the experience levels of the coaches. The lack of experience on the part of the coaches raises concerns about their capacity to support teacher professional growth and instructional improvement. This problem is particularly acute in schools with high teacher turnover and a disproportionate number of underprepared teachers.

Although there are more coaches in such struggling schools, they also tend to work with more teachers. Due to high teacher-to-coach ratios, coaches cannot work deeply with all teachers. Teachers often have to be proactive to get coaching support, and new teachers tend to get more coaching. Overall, some teachers benefit considerably from working with a school-based coach or meeting regularly with colleagues. But when coaches themselves are inexperienced or can work with teachers only superficially because of their competing demands, or when collaborative time is devoured by administrative minutiae, teachers are less positive.

The realities of time in a school also affect teachers' abilities to engage fully in professional development. Responsibilities beyond normal teaching duties also chip away at time for training opportunities. In fact, teachers spend a considerable amount of time supporting others' professional development, perhaps at the expense of their own. Teachers with more than a year of experience report the many ways that they contribute to the development of the teaching profession.

Fragmented programmes and efforts occurring simultaneously in schools also affect teachers' professional development. Even with the narrowing of state professional development opportunities, most teachers experience fragmented training, piecing together various components throughout the year but failing to complete a unified picture.

The disparate professional development offerings send conflicting messages to teachers about what constitutes high-quality and effective instructional practices. Much of the privately funded professional development does not directly support the curriculum adopted by schools. Reflective experienced teachers with sufficient on-site instructional support and the freedom to supplement the curriculum may be better equipped than beginning teachers to resolve the inconsistencies between divergent instructional approaches. For teachers at all levels of experience, workplace conditions can overwhelm even the best-planned professional development.

Teachers can have too many demands on their time. In addition, schools can have so many different programmes operating that professional development becomes confusing and contradictory. In schools and districts with a majority of inexperienced or underprepared teachers, professional development on how to use adopted curricula tends to be appreciated by beginning teachers because of the structure it provides. In these districts, administrators, dealing with large numbers of underprepared teachers and constant staff turnover, design professional development to meet the needs of novice teachers in core academic subjects.

For new teachers or for teachers who have to focus on the mechanics of teaching reading, they needed a programme. They needed a set of guidelines, because they no longer do their own thing. This undifferentiated approach leaves experienced teachers and teachers with atypical assignments, such as special education, with few to no school-based professional development opportunities that they feel meet their needs.

In few districts, teachers possess training and experience in other pedagogical philosophies and are more likely to integrate a variety of curricular and instructional approaches into their teaching. A teacher in a suburban district explained that the district requires her to teach to the standards and use the district-mandated instructional programmes. Teachers rely on other supports to fill in gaps in the initial professional development. The on-site support that teachers receive from coaches better serve their specific needs.

At a rural high school, special education teachers' professional development challenges are further complicated by their lack of contact with mainstream teachers. This situation has been amplified by the increased focus on standards and curriculum alignment. The curriculum alignment activities are conducted by grade level and subject cohorts; special education teachers are at a distinct disadvantage because they are responsible for students from a range of grades and subjects.

Among beginning teachers especially, burdens placed on them by personal pressure to bolster their resumes and accommodate administrative requests compete with professional development for attention. Whether new or experienced, special education teachers struggle to participate in meaningful professional development opportunities.

## Guidelines for Effective Teaching

A teaching portfolio for promotion and tenure should be a succinct document which contains information from a variety of sources. The Teaching Portfolio should provide sufficient evidence for the following criteria:

i) Demonstrated excellence in teaching and learning
ii) Demonstrated leadership in teaching and learning
iii) Commitment to high quality education

***Table 1***

***Evidence of excellence in effective teaching and learning***

| *Item* | *Description* |
|---|---|
| 1. Teaching aims, objectives and practices | Summary of your aims, objectives and practices in teaching and student learning. How you monitor or evaluate student learning. How you identify student difficulties and encourage participation in courses or programmes. Description of student assessment methods and rationales, and feedback to students. How your research help in your teaching methods in supervising postgraduate students. |
| 2. Representative course syllabi | Details of course content, objectives, teaching methods, reading lists, homework assignments, student assessment procedures, reflective statements as to the course construction. |
| 3. Subjects taught and supervised | List of course titles and codes, year, points value, enrolments, hours, level of responsibility, |

*(Contd...)*

*(Contd...)*

| | |
|---|---|
| | and a brief description of the way each course is taught. Number of honours and postgraduate students supervised. Research group activities directed. Schedule of times you are available to students outside class. |
| 4. Course and instructional materials | List and provide examples of quality course materials, manuals, outlines, new projects, assignments, study guides, reading lists and annotated bibliographies. Publication of a textbook or other instructional material. |
| 5. Concurrent related duties | Concurrent teaching related duties and responsibilities, e.g., course coordination. |
| 6. School expectations and resources | Summary statement of your school's policies, expectations and resources in relation to teaching. A statement by the head of school assessing your contribution to the school and how the school plans to use your skills in the future. |
| 7. Teaching awards | Awards for teaching excellence presented by student bodies. These reflect merit, provided that they are officially recognised or have been appropriately referred. Peer recognition and other awards for excellence in teaching or supervision. |

*(Contd...)*

*(Contd...)*

| | |
|---|---|
| 8. Teaching innovations, use of technology and flexible teaching and learning | Examples of innovations designed or adopted and their effectiveness. Description of how audiovisual, computer and other information technology-based materials were used in teaching. Description of flexible learning opportunities made available to students. This might include work carried out as part of a teaching development grant. |
| 9. Course, curriculum or departmental development | Revising, setting up or running a course, programme or internship. contribution to improvement of teaching in your department. |
| 10. Research into teaching | Pursuing research that contributes directly to teaching. |
| 11. Teaching publications | Contributing to a professional journal on teaching in general, or in a specific discipline. |
| 12. Teaching associations | Participating in seminars, workshops and professional meetings intended to improve teaching and learning. |
| 13. Teaching consultancies | Teaching consultancies in outside institutions and agencies or requests for demonstrations of effective teaching methods. |

*(Contd...)*

*(Contd...)*

| | |
|---|---|
| 14. Securing grants | Success at securing grants for teaching-related activities. |
| 15. Assistance to colleagues | Evidence of help given to colleagues on course development or teaching improvement. Professional exchanges with colleagues inside or outside the institution. This might focus on course materials or methods of teaching particular topics. |
| 16. Request for advice | Requests for or acknowledgment of advice given to committees on teaching or similar bodies. |
| 17. Invitations to teach, present or publish. | Invitations from outside institutions and agencies to teach or to demonstrate effective teaching methods. Invitations to present at conferences on topics about teaching. Invitations to contribute to the literature on teaching. |

## References

Clark, T., Hickey, C., & Sacramento, K., "*Approval of professional teacher induction programs*", *Report presented at the meeting of the June 5, 2003*, California Commission on Teacher Credentialing, Sacramento, CA, 2003.

Corcoran, T. B., "*Helping teachers teach well: transforming professional development*", New Brunswick, NJ: Center for Policy Research in Education, Rutgers University, 1995.

Darling-Hammond, L., & McLaughlin, M. W., "Policies that support professional development in an era of reform", *Phi Delta Kappan,* 76(8), 597-604, 1995

Little, J. W., "Teachers' professional development in a climate of educational reform", *Educational Evaluation and Policy Analysis, 15*(2), 129-151, 1993.

Rice, J., *Teacher quality: understanding the effectiveness of teacher attributes,* Washington, DC: Economic Policy Institute, 2003.

Wilson, S. M., Floden, R. E., & Ferrini-Mundy, J., "*Teacher preparation research: Current knowledge, gaps, and recommendations*", Seattle, WA: Center for the Study of Teaching and Policy, 2001.

# 13
# Online Teaching

In recent years, technology specifically in the form of computers and the internet, has become a major focus of education policy and reform. Schools with computer hardware and software, allowed schools and classrooms to connect to the internet, and supported technology-focused professional opportunities for teachers. As the numbers of computers and access to the internet in schools have grown, so have the number of questions being asked about the extent to which these technologies are being used in schools and classrooms and for what purposes.

CD-ROM reference and surfing the internet are more likely to be assigned as classroom activities than games and traditional drill-and-practice applications. However, many of these newer uses have been limited to a small proportion of teachers and students. Teachers are in fact using computers or the internet generally more frequently to complete a number of instruction-related tasks than to augment instruction itself.

These technologies are used to help prepare for classroom instruction (e.g., to access research on best practices, download information to present in class) or to complete administrative tasks (e.g., to record and calculate grades). Teachers may also use technology to communicate with parents or students about students' performance, assignments, or special events. They may also use technology to communicate with other members of their profession to share ideas or strategies for presenting content or helping students who are struggling with the content.

The history of technology use for learning suggests, the way educators teach and students learn has not changed dramatically over the past two decades. The research on teacher change and instructional reform in general indicates that such changes in teacher practice are often slow, minimal, or even non-existent. A number of factors contribute to the success or failure of instructional reforms. One important factor the literature has identified is that teachers do not always have opportunities to learn about and practise instructional reforms.

In the area of technology, teachers may have learned about how to use computers and adapt their teaching from a variety of sources-teacher preparation programmes (for prospective teachers), professional development activities (for practising teachers), and informal learning opportunities such as assistance from classmates, colleagues, or students. Professional development research suggests that teachers' opportunities to learn about education technology during traditional professional development activities are often lacking.

Over the past 20 years, education technology has been a major focus of reform and policy at the federal level, as well as at state and local levels. Such initiatives have been guided by the goals of increasing the availability of computers in classrooms and schools, assisting schools with internet access, and providing resources and guidance for teacher training and the integration of technology into the curriculum. The availability of computers and the internet has increased significantly in the nation's schools and classrooms. This increase has been coupled with initiatives aimed toward understanding how best to use technology to improve teaching and learning, and training educators to use technology effectively.

In the early 1980s, students most often used computers for drill and practice. Typically, drill-and-practice software consists of sequences of worksheet-style questions that automatically adjust their difficulty to match individual students' responses. Also, in the early 1980s, teachers typically used computers to teach students programming skills. They rarely used computers for content-related instruction; students were more likely to learn about how to use computers at school than they were to use computers to learn about mathematics or social studies. By the early 1990s, the practice of using computers for programming had declined considerably, and an emphasis on using computers as a tool for learning content had emerged. However, the primary use of computers remained drill and practice in elementary schools in the early 1990s.

In high schools, it was classes on computer education, and middle schools provided a combination of drill and practice and computer education. Finally, as the decade of the 1990s progressed, school computer use shifted to some degree to reflect a greater emphasis on problem solving and indepth learning and less emphasis on drill and practice and basic skills. Professional development activities in general have been widely criticised for being relatively ineffective. Specifically, they have been described as short term, devoid of continuity due to inadequate follow-up and the lack of ongoing feedback from experts, isolated from the participants' classroom and school contexts, and characterised by too few opportunities to learn by doing and reflecting with colleagues.

In fact, while a majority of teachers participate in such activities, a small percentage of teachers report feeling very well prepared to integrate technology into instruction. Traditional programmes for prospective teachers have been described as fragmented, superficial, and unconnected to real classroom experiences. With respect to education technology, some observers have claimed that prospective teachers are not getting the training they need to successfully integrate technology into classroom instruction. For example, some researchers have reported that most students training to become teachers do not routinely use technology while in the field and do not work under supervising teachers who can advise them on using technology in the classroom.

Additionally, about half of the technology training that prospective teachers get in the classroom is delivered as part of other classes, and the other half is provided in the form of stand-alone technology classes. Furthermore, most teacher-preparation programmes provided by schools, colleges, and departments of education do not have written, funded, regularly updated technology plans. Informal learning opportunities, in addition to these formal learning opportunities, may also provide teachers with assistance using technology. Peer collaboration, in particular, has been heralded by many teachers, researchers, and policy makers as essential for teachers' continuous learning.

Teachers may benefit when they learn about technology from one another and provide one another with motivation to continue working with this resource. Research supports this proposition; teachers who use computers benefit from interacting with a network of other teachers at their school who also use computers.

Specifically, certain characteristics of classrooms and schools, such as equipment, time, technical assistance, and leadership, may act as either barriers to or facilitators of technology use. On a most basic level, teachers may be more likely to integrate computers and the internet into classroom instruction if they have access to adequate equipment and connections. Research indicates that the number of computers in America's classrooms and schools has grown substantially in recent years. In 1983, there was one computer for every 125 students. By 1998, there was one computer for every six students.

Although the presence of computers and the internet has grown sharply in recent years, much of the technology equipment currently in schools and classrooms is from an earlier generation of technology-computers with less processing power, less storage capability, and limited capacity for being linked together electronically.

At the same time, teachers face many other challenges, including rapidly increasing technological changes and a greater diversity in the classroom. With regard to technology, there is often little time in teachers' schedules to become familiar with hardware and software or to learn to integrate the new technology into their lesson plans. Lack of time to become acquainted with technology and learn to use it has been identified as the greatest obstacle to the effective use of education technology.

Another important resource for the development of teacher expertise in the use of education technology is technical assistance. A full-time computer coordinator, for example, may assist teachers with using computer software and hardware or adapting their teaching practice to include computer or internet use.

Principal leadership has been described as one of the most important factors affecting the effective use of technology in classrooms. Principals who exhibit leadership are instrumental in modelling the use of technology in classrooms. They understand how it can support best practices in instruction and assessment and provide teachers with guidance for its use. Principals may also participate actively in professional development activities related to education technology and provide teachers with opportunities to learn how to use these resources.

Elementary teachers were more likely than secondary teachers to use the computer or internet to communicate with parents at home, use the computer or internet for classroom instruction, assign projects inside the classroom, or assign students to use computers to practice drills or to solve problems and analyse data. On the other hand, secondary teachers were more likely than elementary teachers to use computers or the internet for administrative record keeping at home and school, as well as communicating with students at school, assigning projects outside of class, and assigning students to conduct research using the internet.

Teachers in low minority and low poverty schools were generally more likely than teachers in high minority and high poverty schools, respectively, to use computers or the internet for a wide range of activities, including gathering information at school, creating instructional materials at school, communicating with colleagues at school, and instructing students. Teachers with the fewest years of experience were more likely than teachers with the most years of experience to use computers or the internet to gather information for planning lessons and creating instructional materials at home. They were also generally more likely than more experienced teachers to use these technologies to access research and best practices examples at school and model lesson plans at school and at home.

Teachers' use of technology for preparatory and administrative purposes varied by a number of school and teacher characteristics. For example, among teachers with computers available in their schools, secondary teachers were more likely than elementary teachers to use computers or the internet at school for administrative record keeping, and they were also more likely to do this at home than elementary teachers. Moreover, teachers in schools with the fewest students enrolled were more likely than teachers in schools with the highest enrolments to use these technologies at school to gather information for planning lessons.

Teachers' use of technology for communicative purposes varied by a number of school and teacher characteristics. For example, elementary teachers were more likely than secondary teachers to use computers or the internet at home to communicate with parents. On the other hand, secondary teachers were more likely than elementary teachers to use these technologies at school to communicate with students.

Furthermore, teachers in schools with medium-sized enrolments were more likely than teachers in schools with small enrolments to report that they used computers or the internet at home to communicate with colleagues. Teachers in schools with large enrollments were also more likely to use these technologies at school to post homework or assignments and at home to conduct this task.

## Development of Competencies

Information technology is changing the way people live and learn. Information technology (IT) is also transforming the nature of teaching. These remarks provide a framework for thinking about such changes and exploring work in progress that is relevant to the development of competencies specific to teaching online. Competence refers to a state of being well qualified to perform an activity, task or job function. When a person is competent to do something, he or she has achieved a state of competence that is recognizable and verifiable to a particular community of practitioners. A competency, then, refers to the way that a state of competence can be demonstrated to the relevant community.

According to the International Board of Standards for Training, Performance and Instruction (IBSTPI), a competency involves a related set of knowledge, skills and attitudes that enable a person to effectively perform the activities of a given occupation or function in such a way that meets or exceeds the standards expected in a particular profession or work setting. The structure and assessment of competencies may differ from one community of practice to another and even within a community. To facilitate a common understanding of competencies in the context of online and distributed learning some specifications have been elaborated.

Typically, a competency is divided into specific indicators describing the requisite knowledge, skills, attitudes and context of performance. There are different ways to validate that a person has demonstrated the relevant competencies. Teacher certification is a common practice, and the notion of teacher competencies is fairly well established. However, competencies are generally associated with highly formalised professional activities and not applied to ill-defined tasks.

Ill-defined tasks certainly include many forms of teaching. This narrow view of competence runs counter to common sense and professional practice, but brings into attention the mainstream approach to elaboration of teacher competencies where it is essential to clearly identify the conditions of teaching. The delivery environment (classroom-based, internet-based, laboratory-based, hybrid environments, and so on) is a particularly relevant condition to identify competencies for online teaching.

The range of activities available in online settings and the multiple conditions of time in which they take place are evidence that the technology demands placed on online teachers are somewhat more significant than those associated with classroom teachers. Much of what has already been published with regard to online teaching has focused on technical skills and requirements of successfully moderating and facilitating online discussions and chat sessions.

In online asynchronous discussions, the moderator's competencies involve:

i) allowing learners time for reflection,
ii) keeping discussions alive and on a productive path, and
iii) archiving and organising discussions to be used in subsequent lessons.

In online synchronous discussions (e.g., chat), the moderator must:

i) establish ground rules for discussion,
ii) animate interactions with minimal instructor intervention,
iii) sense how online text messages may appear to distant learners, and
iv) be aware of cultural differences.

At the environment level, however, the ways in which a teacher demonstrates such competence is quite different, which suggests that there are competencies unique to online settings. Teaching competencies and online teaching competencies have generally been considered separately.

The current interest in competencies for online teaching is coming from business and industry, primarily with regard to technical training and professional development courses offered in online settings. It is quite likely that some of the interest in competencies for online teaching is a result of hastily-crafted online courses and inadequate preparation of online facilitators.

Clearly technology offers the potential to create and implement highly engaging and effective online environments to support a wide variety of learning goals. It is also quite clear that the capacity to make effective use of information technology in educational settings is impaired by inadequate preparation of teachers (as well as learners) and by a shortage of properly trained instructional designers and educational support personnel. The development of competencies for online teaching should lead to the associated development of training for online teachers and (in some cases) to the certification of online teachers.

To develop competencies for online teachers is not without challenge. Competencies are dynamic in nature, and they largely depend on the relevant social context. The constant transformation of IT makes the development of competencies for online teachers a continuous process and demands continuing professional preparation and training for online teachers. Such endeavours will improve the ability to make effective use of technology in learning and instruction.

## Online Teaching Assessment

Assessment plays an important part in the learning process—both summative and formative assessments inform progress and guide learning; it is essential to the accreditation process; and, results are used in all sorts of ways to measure outcomes and success of the student, teacher, course, or institute. Self-assessment encourages student independence, and helps students develop the necessary skills for autonomous (and lifelong) learning. Assessment, especially when embedded within an 'authentic' learning tasks or exercises, can also be an essential part of the learning experience. Principal reasons why online assessment is of fundamental importance are:

i) Student learning and behaviour is affected by and often led by assessment requirements.

ii) When designing learning programmes, the assessment criteria and assessment constraints are usually key determinants of the teaching and learning strategies chosen. If teachers are to engage in new forms of teaching and take advantage of the greatly enhanced teaching options now possible through online and mixed-mode teaching then it stands to reason that we need to unpack assessment options and issues if online teaching and learning is to be maximised.

iii) Effective flexible learning regimes require assessment to be appropriately designed to match the new learning environments and diverse clientele.

iv) There is a new wave of pedagogy advocating 'alternative assessment' in which assessment is integrated with learning processes and real-life performance as opposed to display of 'inert knowledge'.

Known as 'authentic assessment' it is very much based on the constructivist approach that enables students to demonstrate knowledge by working on authentic tasks, putting students in control of their own learning. Constructivism is a theory of learning that advocates that students construct meaning through active participation with the environment and with others, incorporating new information with existing knowledge.

Online assessment like other forms of assessment needs to be valid, reliable, fair, and flexible. Further, it is a requirement for training and assessment to be equitable for all persons, taking account of cultural and linguistic needs. Assessment should be sufficiently flexible and diverse to account for differing needs and circumstance of students undertaking online study. Flexibility can mean:

i) providing assessment choices

ii) negotiating assessment tasks to account for student's circumstances and needs

iii) providing flexibility in timeliness or providing contingency options to cater for unreliability or differences in technology connections in providing choice in location of assessment as students do assessment tasks in their place of study which can be home, work or wherever they choose, providing supervision is not required.

The extent to which these choices are available in online learning depends on many factors, including pragmatic issues of managing learning and learners, teaching strategies employed, requirements to start and finish on given dates and so forth.

Key issues for the online learning context are:

i) Identifying what assessment methods can effectively be transferred to or be done better or differently online
ii) Identifying whether and how the medium and mode impacts upon the validity, reliability, fairness, and flexibility of assessment
iii) Identifying the barriers to using online assessment
iv) Understanding whether and how online changes, how we select, monitor, and manage assessment activities.
v) Authentication for summative assessments.

Assessment for online is underpinned by the same principles of validity, reliability, flexibility and fairness, and uses many of the same strategies used in traditional face-to-face teaching. What differs mostly is the context of the assessment, the interactions between assessor and those being assessed, and collection and administration processes. Online can be used:

i) as a stand-alone source of evidence for assessment
ii) as a contribution to the total assessment process or for the collection, transmission and administration of assessment materials and resources.

Online assessment can provide:

i) greater flexibility in where, when, and how assessment is undertaken

ii) students with a greater range of options to demonstrate their knowledge and skills.

Assessment can be by: teacher, self, peer, or by an external person or group. Online assessment, like online teaching, is still very much in an embryonic state. The most common online assessment strategies are: using computer communications as a transfer medium to submit and comment upon assigned work such as essays; compiling and submitting portfolios; and for computer testing, i.e., short answer, multiple choice type questions and quizzes. There is growing interest in communication tools for learning interactions and evidence that this can work well, but the use of conferencing and online group work as assessable activities is not yet widespread.

Online does not as yet lend itself easily to the testing of competencies that require the demonstration of a particular skill or work-based task. Both summative and formative assessment have very important roles to play in flexible learning. Currently online is used more for 'summative' assessment than for formative assessment.

"Authentic" online assessment that is integrated with the learning experience, not separated from it, is considered to be one of the most effective ways of measuring student's learning. According to Anderson it promotes skills transfer and deeper level understandings—'learners are assessed within a relevant context and are required to collaborate extensively to produce a product that demonstrates the knowledge, understanding and skills they have learned, and the ability to manage activities.

Communication and interaction are essential elements within learning. There are views that 'required' participation and input into online discussion forums, chats, emails, face-to-face seminars provides tangible benefit to the learner and impacts upon learning outcomes; it helps keep learners motivated and involved; enables students to support each other's learning; and provides opportunities for peer and teacher feedback to individuals and student groups. Some have found from experience that unless participation is assessable, students do not feel compelled to participate, hence reducing the effectiveness for others.

Another difficulty for teachers is authentication—knowing that the person participating is in fact the person they profess to be. Online technologies can provide the means to track and record student work and conversations. Extreme care needs to be taken to ensure that privacy and confidentiality requirements are observed and that the learning environment is established in a way that students feel comfortable and confident to work in the online setting. Other areas of simultaneous opportunity and challenge afforded by online teaching is that of peer and student self-assessment.

As with group assignments in traditional face-to-face on-campus teaching, online assessment requires the selection of appropriate and defendable assessment criteria. Assessment might be of the product or output of the group work, on process only, or a mixture of both. With online assessments consideration also needs to be given to disadvantages that may occur because of student access to technology.

Authentication and plagiarism are topics of great concern to teachers and sceptics of online teaching. There are two types of plagiarism: intended copying of direct passages of other people's work and ideas without acknowledgement, and, lack of acknowledgement through poor or incorrect referencing techniques. The latter points to the need for inclusion of instruction and guides on referencing to include the need to acknowledge sources obtained from the web and the correct ways of acknowledging online material.

Issues of security in online assessment most often relate to:

i) dependability and reliability of systems so that students (and teachers) are not disadvantaged if systems fail or have downtime

ii) integrity of data of online systems

iii) prevention and tracking of unauthorised access.

Teachers and students need to be assured that adequate security is in place. The importance of management support cannot be overstressed. Assessment strategies and tasks should be aligned to the learning objectives and learning process, and the connection should be made explicit to students so that they can see the relevance of the assessment to the learning task.

When developing online assessment it is recommended that teachers and practitioners consult with others on the nature of the assessment task to ensure the assessment is valid, viable, and authentic. Online learning by its very nature requires a degree of independence in students and the ability to problem solve (that is, the ability to solve learning problems as well as technical problems).

Self-assessment, peer assessment, discovery learning, reflection and articulation are just some of the ways students are being encouraged to manage their own learning. Other ways include options to negotiate assessment activities, mode of presentation, timing of assessment, and decisions about grading or mark allocations. The challenge remains as always though to find measurable evidence to show attainment of competencies and desired attributes.

**Barriers to Online Assessment**

Barriers to effective use of online assessment identified by Paulsen in an international study to inform decision makers included: public and institutional regulations, traditions for physical attendance, technical limitations, student identification, and detection of plagiarised digital material. Clearly technology lends itself better to some forms of assessment than to others, but mostly barriers often relate to teachers knowing sufficient about the available options and being able to confidently connect the appropriate assessment options to the different teaching and learning strategies they might employ.

Teachers also need to feel confident they can overcome some of the issues associated with online assessment. The pragmatics of time, available resources, cost, and lack of support are also often listed as barriers. Or at the very least electronic communications have impacted very significantly on teaching and learning options which in turn will challenge traditional assessment regimes.

As well, online assessment techniques will broaden and be refined as technical capabilities expand, access becomes less problematic, and the status of teaching, learning and assessment online matures. As online learning becomes more mainstream, providers recognise that online learning is an option in all teaching and not something to be accounted for separately, assessment systems will be integrated with other student management systems and business processing.

## References

Becker, H. J., "School uses of microcomputers: Report #1 from a national survey", *Journal of Computers in Mathematics and Science Teaching*, 3(2), 29-33, 1983.

Becker, H. J., "Instructional uses of school computers", *Reports from the 1985 National Survey*, Issue No. 3. Baltimore, MD: Johns Hopkins University, Center for Social Organisation of Schools, 1986.

Becker, H. J., "When powerful tools meet conventional beliefs and institutional constraints", *The Computing Teacher*, 18(8), 6-9, 1991.

Calderhead, J., "Teachers: Beliefs and knowledge", In D. Berliner & R. Calfee (Eds.), *Handbook of Educational Psychology* (pp. 709-725), New York: Simon & Schuster Macmillan, 1996.

Cyrs, T., "Competence in teaching at a distance", *New Directions for Teaching and Learning, 71,* 15-18, 1997.

Collison, G., Elbaum, B., Haavind, S., & Tinker, R., *Facilitating online learning: Effective strategies for moderators,* Madison, WI: Atwood Publishing, 2000.

Goodyear, P., "Online teaching", In N. Hativa & P. Goodyear (Eds.), *Teacher thinking, beliefs and knowledge in higher education*, Dordrecht: Kluwer, 2000.

_______________ , Salmon, G., Spector, M., Steeples, C., & Tickner, S., "Competencies for online teaching", *Educational Technology Research & Development 49* (1), 65-72, 2001.

Kearsely, G., *Online education: Learning and teaching in cyberspace,* Belmont, CA: Wadsworth, 2000

Rosenberg, M. J., *E-learning: Strategies for delivering knowledge in the digital age,* New York: McGraw Hill, 2001.

Schoenfeld-Tacher, R., & Persichitte, K., "Differential skills and com-petencies required of faculty teaching distance education courses", *International Journal of Educational Technology, 2* (1), 2000.

# Bibliography

Allinder, R. M., "The relationships between efficacy and the instructional practices of special education teachers and consultants", *Teacher Education and Special Education*, 17, 86-95, 1994.

Anderson, R, Greene, M., & Loewen, P., "Relationships among teachers' and students' thinking skills, sense of efficacy, and student achievement", *Alberta Journal of Educational Research*, 34(2), 148-165, 1988.

Arendale, David, *Bridging the Gap of Teaching and Learning*, University of Missouri—Kansas City, 1997.

Atin, A. W. and Chang, M. J., "Colleges that emphasise research and reaching, can you have your cake and eat it too?", *Change*, pp. 45- 49, 1995.

Ayersman, D., "Reviewing the research on hypermedia-based learning", *Journal of Research on Computing in Education*, 28:4, 500-525, 1996.

Bakker, G., "Using 'pedagogical-impact statements' to make teaching and research symbiotic activities", *Chronicle of Higher Education*, 17 March, p. B3, 1995.

Bandura, A., *Social foundations of thought and action: A social cognitive theory*, Englewood Cliffs, NJ: Prentice-Hall, 1986.

Bareth, L. G. & Manning, M.L., *Multicultural Education of Children and Adolescents*, Needham Heights, MA: Allyn and Bacon, 1992.

Barnett, R., "Linking teaching and research, a critical inquiry", *Journal of Higher Education*, 63(6), pp. 619- 636, 1992.

Barnett, R., "Linking Teaching and Research", *Journal of Higher Education*, Vol. 63, No. 6, pp. 619-636, 1992.

Barnett, W. S., "Long-term effects of early childhood programs on cognitive and school outcomes", *Future of Children*, 5(3), 25 - 50, 1995.

Barron, L. C., Goldman, E. S., "Integrating technology with teacher preparation", In B. Means (Ed.), *Technology and Education Reform* (pp. 57-81). San Francisco, CA: Jossey-Bass, 1994.

Bassey, M, and Constable, H., "Higher education research in education 1992 to 1996: fields of enquiry reported in the RAE", *Research Intelligence*, 61, BERA, July, 1977.

Batty, M., and Mathews, S. A., "Relationship between teaching and research?", *Area*, 20, pp. 158-162, 1988.

Bayraktar, S., "A Meta-analysis of the effectiveness of computer-assisted instruction in science education", *Journal of Research on Technology in Education* 34:3, 173-188, 2002.

Becker, H. J., "Instructional uses of school computers", *Reports from the 1985 National Survey*, Issue No. 3. Baltimore, MD: Johns Hopkins University, Center for Social Organisation of Schools, 1986.

Becker, H. J., "School uses of microcomputers: Report #1 from a national survey", *Journal of Computers in Mathematics and Science Teaching*, 3(2), 29-33, 1983.

_______________ , Wong, Y., "Teacher and teacher-directed student use of computers and software", *Report #3. Teaching Learning and Computing: 1998 National Survey*, Irvine, CA: University of California at Irvine, Center for Research in Information Technology in Organizations, 1999

Bee, H., *The Developing Child, Fourth Edition*, New York: Harper and Row, 1985.

Berson, M., "Effectiveness of computer technology in the social studies: A Review of the literature", *Journal of Research on Computing in Education*, 28:4, 486-499, 1996.

Biggs, J.B., *Teaching for Quality Learning at University: What the Student Does, Open University Press*, Milton Keynes, 1999.

Bley, N.S., Thornton, C.A., *Teaching mathematics to students with learning disabilities* (3rd ed.), Austin, TX: Pro-Ed, 1995.

Blok, H., Oostdam, R., Otter, M. and Overmaat, M., "Computer-assisted instruction in support of beginning reading instruction: A review", *Review of Educational Research*, 72:1, 101-130, 2002.

Bowman, B., "Kindergarten practices for children from low income homes", In R. Pianta & M. Cox, Eds., *The transition to kindergarten*, Baltimore, MD: Paul H. Brookes, 1999.

Boyer, E.L., Teaching's renewed role in evaluation of learning, *Times Higher Education Supplement*, 1990

Branca, N., Breedlove, B., King, B., "Calculators in the middle grades: Access to rich mathematics", In J.T. Fey & C.R. Hirsch (Eds.), *Calculators in mathematics education: 1992 yearbook*, Reston, VA: National Council of Teachers of Mathematics, 1992.

Bresler, J.B., "Teaching Effectiveness and Government Awards", *Science, Vol.160*, pp. 164-167, 1968.

Brew, A. & Boud, D., "Research and Learning in Higher Education", in Research, Teaching and Learning in Higher Education, eds B. Smith & S. Brown, Kogan Page, London, pp. 30-39, 1995.

Brew, A., "Research and teaching: changing relationships in a changing context", *Studies in Higher Education*, 24(3), pp. 291-391, 1999.

Brown, G and Atkins, M., *Effective Teaching in Higher Education,* Methuen, London, 1988.

Calderhead, J., "Teachers: Beliefs and knowledge", In D. Berliner & R. Calfee (Eds.), *Handbook of Educational Psychology* (pp. 709-725), New York: Simon & Schuster Macmillan, 1996.

Carrasquillo, A., *Hispanic children and youth in the United States: A Resource Guide*, New York: Garland, 1991.

Carter, K., "Using cases to frame mentor-novice conversations about teaching", *Theory Into Practice,* 27. 214-222/, 1989.

Cena, Johanna E., Bridging Gaps Between Cultures, Classrooms and Schools: A Close Look at Online Collaborative Learning, *Educational Technology & Society* 3(3) 2000.

Chickering, A. W. and Gamson, Z. F., "Seven Principles of Good Practice in Undergraduate Education", *AAHE Bulletin*, 39, 3-7, 1987.

Christensen, D. H., "The Use of Qualitative Methods in Family and Consumer Sciences: A Reflection", *Family and Consumer Sciences Research Journal 27*, no. 4, June 1999.

Clark, B.R., "The modern integratio n of research activities with teaching and learning", *Journal of Higher Education*, 68(3), pp. 242- 255, 1997.

Clark, T., Hickey, C., & Sacramento, K., "*Approval of professional teacher induction programs*", *Report presented at the meeting of the June 5, 2003*, California Commission on Teacher Credentialing, Sacramento, CA, 2003.

Cochran-Smith, M, and Lytle, S., "Research on teaching and teacher research: The issues that divide", *Educational Researcher*, 19, 2-11, 1990.

Coladarci, T., "Teachers' sense of efficacy and commitment to teaching", *Journal of Experimental Education*, 60, 323-337, 1992.

Collison, G., Elbaum, B., Haavind, S., & Tinker, R., *Facilitating online learning: Effective strategies for moderators,* Madison, WI: Atwood Publishing, 2000.

Corcoran, T. B., "*Helping teachers teach well: transforming professional development*", New Brunswick, NJ: Center for Policy Research in Education, Rutgers University, 1995.

Corno, L., "Encouraging Students to Take Responsibility for Learning and Performance", *The Elementary School Journal* 93(1): 69-84, 1992.

Cox, B.G, and Ramirez, M., "Cognitive styles: Implications for multiethnic education", In J. Banks, (Ed.), *Education in the 80's: Implications for multiethnic education*, Washington, DC: National Education Association, 1981.

Creswell, J. W., *Qualitative Inquiry and Re-search Design: Choosing among Five Traditions*, Thousand Oaks, CA: Sage, 1998.

Cuban, L., *Teachers and machines: The classroom uses of technology since 1920*, New York: Teachers College Press, 1986.

Cyrs, T., "Competence in teaching at a distance", *New Directions for Teaching and Learning, 71,* 15-18, 1997.

Dalton, B., Morocco, C.C., Tivnan, T., & Mead, P.L.R., "Supported inquiry science: Teaching for conceptual change in urban and suburban science classrooms", *Journal of Learning Disabilities, 30*(6), 670-684, 1997.

Darling-Hammond, L., & McLaughlin, M. W., "Policies that support professional development in an era of reform", *Phi Delta Kappan, 76*(8), 597-604, 1995

Downes, Toni, Andrew Fluck, Pam Gibbons, Ralph Leonard, Caroline Matthews, Ron Oliver, Margaret Vickers and Michelle Williams, *Making Better Connections:Models of teacher professional development for the integration of information and communication technology into classroom practice*, Department of Education,Training and Youth Affairs, Canberra, 2001.

Dynarski, Mark, Margaret Honey, Doug Levin, "Designing A Study of the Effectiveness of Education Technology", *Background Material for the First Meeting of the Technical Working Group*, 1996.

Eisner, E., *The Enlightened Eye: Qualitative Inquiry and the Enhancement of Educa-tional Practice*, New York: Macmillan, 1991.

Elton, L and Partington, P., *Teaching Standards and Excellence in Higher Education Developing a Culture for Quality*, 2nd edn, CVCP/USD, Sheffield, 1993.

_______________ , *Research and teaching: what are the real relationships*? (forthcoming)", 1999.

Ennis, R.H., "A Taxonomy of Critical Thinking Dispositions and Abilities", In J.B. Baron and R.S. Sternberg, Eds, *Teaching Thinking Skills: Theory and Practice*, Hillsdale, NJ: Lawrence Erlbaum Associates, 1987

Everett, D., "Marketing education assessment guide", *Performance-based activities with authentic assessment instruments,* Columbia, MO: Missouri University, Instructional materials laboratory, 1997.

Finson, K.D., Ormsbee, C.K., "Rubrics and their use in inclusive science", *Intervention in School and Clinic, 34*(2), 79-88, 1998.

Fitzgerald, G. and Koury, K., "Empirical advances in technology-assisted instruction for students with mild and moderate disabilities", *Journal of Research on Computing in Education*, 28:4, 526-553, 1996.

Foote, K.E., "Bringing faculty on-line; inspiring and sustaining innovation in information and computer technologies (ICT)", *Journal of Geography in Higher Education*, 23(1), pp. 5- 8, 1999.

Garman, N., "Qualitative Inquiry: Meaning and Menace for Educational Researchers", In *Qualitative Research Practice in Adult Education*, edited by P. Willis and B. Neville, pp. 11-29. Ringwood, Victoria, Australia: David Lovell Publishing, 1996.

Gay, G., "Multicultural infusiou in teacher education, Foundations and applications", *Peabody Journal of Education*, 72(l), 150-177, 1997.

Golafshani, Nahid, Understanding Reliability and Validity in Qualitative Research, *The Qualitative Report,* University of

Toronto, Toronto, Ontario, Canada, Volume 8, Number 4 December 2003.

Gollnick, D.M, & and Chin, P.C., *Multicultural education in a pluralistic society (5 th edition)*, New Jersey: Prentice Hall, 1998.

Goodyear, P., "Online teaching", In N. Hativa & P. Goodyear (Eds.), *Teacher thinking, beliefs and knowledge in higher education*, Dordrecht: Kluwer, 2000.

Gregson, J. A., "Editorial: Reflecting on Qualitative Research and Vocational Education", *Journal of Vocational Education Research 23*, no. 4 (1998): 265-270.

Guskey, T. R., "Teacher efficacy, self-concept, and attitudes toward the implementation of instructional innovation", *Teaching and Teacher Education*, 4, 63-69, 1988.

Harasim, L., "Online education: The future", In T. M. Harrison, & T. Stephen (Eds.), *Computer networking and scholarly communication in the twenty-first-century university*, New York: State University of New York Press, 1996.

Hargreaves, D. H., "Teaching as a Research-based Profession: possibilities and prospects", *Teacher Training Agency Annual Lecture,* 1996.

Hennessy, S., *The potential of portable technologies for supporting graphing investigations*, Institute of Educational Technology, Open University, UK, 1998.

Hoepfl, M. C., "Choosing Qualitative Research: A Primer for Technology Education Researchers", *ln Journal of Technology Education 9*, no. 1: 47-63, 1997

Hounsell, D., "Documenting and assessing excellent teachers, in Evaluating Teacher Quality in Higher Education", ed. R. Aylett and K. Gregory, Falmer, London, 1996.

Howes, C., Phillips D, Whitebook, M., "Thresholds of quality: implications for the social development of children in center-based child care", *Child Development, 63,* 449 - 460, 1992.

Jenkins, Alan, *The Relationship Between Teaching and Research: where does geography stand and deliver*, Oxfor University, UK, Journal of Geography in Higher Education, Vol. 24. No. 3, 2000

Jonassen, D.H., *Computers in the classroom. Mindtools for critical thinking*", Englewood Cliffs, NJ: Prentice-Hall, 1996.

Jones, T. and Paolucci, R., "The learning effectiveness of educational technology: A call for further research", *Educational Technology Review,* 9:10-14,1998

Katz, L.G., "Dispositions in Early Childhood Education" *ERIC/EECE, Bulletin* 18(2): 1-3, 1985.

Kearsely, G., *Online education: Learning and teaching in cyberspace,* Belmont, CA: Wadsworth, 2000

Knight, P.G., "The relationship between teaching and research", Area, 19, pp. 350-352, 1987.

Kober, N., *Edtalk: What we know about science teaching and learning,* Washington, DC: Council for Educational Development and Research, 1991.

Lechner S.K., Lechner K.M, Thomas G.A., "Evalua-tion of a computer aided learning program in prosthodontics", *J Prosthodont* 1999:7 (2):100-105.

Lee, J., "Effectiveness of computer-based instructional simulation: A meta-analysis", *International Journal of Instructional Media,* 26:1, 71-85, 1999.

Little, J. W., "Teachers' professional development in a climate of educational reform", *Educational Evaluation and Policy Analysis, 1*5(2), 129-151, 1993.

Liu, M., Moore, Z., Graham, L., and Lee, S., "A look at the research on computer-based technology use in second-language learning: A review of the literature from 1990-2000", *Journal of Research on Technology in Education* 34:3, 250-273, 2002.

Long A.F., Mercer P.E., Stephens C.D. et al, "The evaluation of three computer-assisted learning packages for general dental practitioners", *Brit Dent J* 1994;177:410-5

Lovitt, T.C., Horton, S.V., "Strategies for adapting science textbooks for youth with learning disabilities", *Remedial and Special Education, 1*5(2), 105-116, 1994.

Mulligan R., Wood G.J., "A controlled evalua-tion of computer assisted training simulations in geriatric dentistry", *J Dent Educ* 1993.

Pajares, F., "Current directions in self-efficacy research", In M. Maehr & P. R. Pintrich (Eds.), *Advances in motivation and achievement* (Vol. 10, pp. 1-49), Greenwich, CT: JAI Press, 1997.

Pianta, R. and Cox, M., Eds., *Transition to kindergarte*n, Baltimore, MD: Brookes Publishing Co., 1999.

Powell, D., *Strengthening parental contributions to school readiness,* Washington, DC: U.S. Department of Education, Office of Educational Research and Improvement, 1991.

Ramirez, M., & Castañeda, A., *Cultural democracy, bicognitive development and education*, p. 169-170. New York: Academic Press, 1974.

Ramsey, Gregor, *Quality Matters—Revitalising Teaching: Critical Times, Critical Choices*, News South Wales Department of Education and Training, Sydney, 2000.

Ravitz, J., "Demystifying data about technology impacts in schools", Paper presented at the National Educational Computing Conference (NECC), San Antonio, TX, June, 2002.

Reed, W.M., "Assessing the impact of computer-based writing instruction", *Journal of Research on Computing in Education,* 28:4, 418-437, 1996.

Rice, J., *Teacher quality: understanding the effectiveness of teacher attributes,* Washington, DC: Economic Policy Institute, 2003.

Riehl, L., Young, V., *Final report of the independent evaluation of the Beginning Teacher Support and Assessment Program (BTSA*), San Francisco, CA: WestEd, 2002.

Rosenberg, M. J., *E-learning: Strategies for delivering knowledge in the digital age,* New York: McGraw Hill, 2001.

Sefton A., "Evaluating the new technologies", *Proceedings of Evaluating New Teaching Technologies,* Uniserve Science, Sydney.

Shipman, S.L., "Limitations of Applying Cognitive Styles to Early Childhood Education", *Early Child Development and Care* (51): 13-28, 1989.

Shneiderman, B., *Designing the user interface: Strategies for effective human-computer-interaction*, Addison Wesley Longman, 1998.

Shonkoff, J, Phillips, D., *From neurons to neighborhoods: The science of early childhood development,* Washington, DC: National Academy Press, 2000.

Shulman, L., "Knowledge and teaching: Foundations of the new reform", *Harvard Educational Review*, 57(1), 1-22, 1987.

Smith Jr. Albert J., *Authentic Assessment Advances Contextual Teaching and Learning*, University of Washington Seattle, Washington, Talking Paper Series Paper #1.01, October, 2000

Snow, C.E., Burns, M.S, Griffin, P., Eds. *Preventing reading difficulties in young childre*n, Washington, DC: National Academy Press, 1998.

Terry, C., Pantle, T., "Authentic assessment: Reducing the fear and trembling", *ERIC Digest*, ERIC Clearinghouse on Tests, Measurement and Evaluation, Washington, D.C., 1994.

Tharp, R., "Culturally compatible education: A formula for designing effective classrooms", In H. Trueba, G. Spindler, & L. Spindler (Eds.), *What do anthropologists have to say about dropouts*? New York: Falmer Press, 1989.

________________ "Psychocultural variables and constants: Effects on teaching and learning in schools", *American Psychologist*, 44, (2), 349-359, February, 1989.

Vavrus, Michael, *The Multicultural Challenge of Racism and the Pedagogical Opportunity of Contextual Teaching & Learning*, 2001.

Weller, H., "Assessing the impact of computer-based learning in science", *Journal of Research on Computing in Education* 28:4, 461-485, 1996.

Wilkes M, Bligh J., "Evaluating educational in-terventions", *Brit Med J* 1999; 318:1269-1272.

Wilson, S. M., Floden, R. E., & Ferrini-Mundy, J., "*Teacher preparation research: Current knowledge, gaps, and recommendations*", Seattle, WA: Center for the Study of Teaching and Policy, 2001.

# Index